IMAGES
of Wales

AROUND
PONTAI

THE SECOND

CH00555715

Aerial photograph of Pontardawe, 1952. The steel and tinplate works lie to the centre right with the sheetworks to the left. The proposed route of Lon Tanyrallt (opened in 1953) can clearly be seen (top right) as can the line of the former Primrose Colliery tramroad, running from top centre, right. Immediately to the left and right of the tramroad, at its 'terminus', are the former chemical works and Ynysfechan colliery sites, respectively. The canal weaves its way through the town while other features include the works pond, Brynheulog (bottom left) and Craig y Adar (bottom right).

IMAGES
of Wales

AROUND
PONTARDAWE

THE SECOND SELECTION

Compiled by

The Pontardawe Historians

Jeff Childs
Roland Murdoch
Clive Reed
Eurig Roberts
Keri Thomas
Eunice Williams
Gordon Williams

TEMPUS

Tempus Publishing Limited
The Mill, Brimscombe Port,
Stroud, Gloucestershire, GL5 2QG

ISBN 0 7524 1655 3

Typesetting and origination by
Tempus Publishing Limited
Printed in Great Britain by
Midway Clark Printing, Wiltshire

Ladies of St John the Baptist's church, Alltwen, *c.* 1930. Those identified are, from left to right, middle row: Mrs Wilde (first), Margaret Jane Gummery (fourth), Iris Jones (fifth) and David Price (eleventh). The Revd Mr Davies is seated.

Contents

Cwmdu waterfalls at Ynysmeudwy, *c.* 1925. The falls are approximately 35 feet high and are situated on the Cwmdu stream or Nant Cwmdu. The stream is formed of numerous issues and un-named watercourses which drain the western slopes of the Gwrhyd mountain. Historically, the stream forms the boundary between the districts of Alltygrug and Mawr and is also the boundary between the villages of Ynysmeudwy and Cilmaengwyn today. Pictured are Hopkin John of Ynysmeudwy Uchaf Farm (wearing the bowler hat) and Mr Witt.

Foreword

Charles Lamb took great pride in the place of his birth. 'I was born' he said, 'under the shadow of St Dunstan's steeple…The same day which gave me to the world, saw London happy in the celebration of her great annual feast. This I cannot help looking upon as a lively omen of the future goodwill which I was destined to bear toward the city.'

Gwenallt, one of Wales' most eminent poets, was born 100 years ago in Wesley Terrace, Pontardawe, and although the greater part of his life was spent outside the Swansea Valley, he, like Lamb, was proud of his birthplace. He once said in a recorded talk 'Rwy'n falch I mi gael fy ngeni ym Mhontardawe' ('I'm glad that I was born in Pontardawe'). Many of us share the same sentiment. Unlike Gwenallt, however, I was fortunate enough not only to have been born in Pontardawe – in a council house in Allt-y-werin – but also to have spent my whole life in the village, apart from two short years in far-off Brynaman!

The Pontardawe of my upbringing was very different in many respects from the Pontardawe of today, and in spite of the fact that my childhood was darkened by the shadows of the Depression and the Second World War I cannot but feel that they were good days. The landscape nowadays is greener and healthier, but there is a warm and comforting nostalgia in one's recollection of tall, smoke-belching stacks, the clanking of buffers as grimy engines hauled their cargo of tinplate across the level crossing near the Gwachel, nights noisy with the tapping of furnaces in Gilbertson's steelworks, and the bodies of unwanted cats and dogs in weighted sacks compounding the pollution of the already polluted canal where we fished with jampots for undernourished tiddlers. We had no chlorinated bathing pool, but we had the Boys' Pond in Cwm Du and the vitriol tainted water of Llyn y Felin which by some inexplicable linguistic contortions we pronounced Sindereli! And we as boys – each one of us replicating Richmal Crompton's William Brown – were so proud during the war of the incendiary bomb casings we collected with the same devotion as our grandparents had collected bits of Swansea porcelain. Our proudest boast was that we hadn't dived under the kitchen table when Pontardawe's one and only high explosive bomb landed harmlessly in the marshy ground 100 yards north of the Foundry. Yes, those – as Mary Hopkin used to sing so sweetly – *Those were the days*. And we are grateful to diligent local historians for reminding us, in published collections of archive material, of our often forgotten past and helping us to recognise again the face of a community which made us what we are. The first volume of *Around Pontardawe* was not just another contribution to the thriving nostalgia industry; it was a valuable photographic record of our past, and I look forward to the pleasure of spending many hours between the pages of this second volume – pages which will bring back some, at least, of our yesterdays. We cannot be sure about tomorrow. But yesterday is safe. We've been there.

Diolch I bawb fu'n gyfrifol am baratoi'r ail gyfrol hon o luniau. Gwerthfawrogwn eu llafur, ac am roi I ni'r pleser o gofio cymaint o bethau y gellid yn hawdd eu hanghofio.

Dafydd Rowlands
Archdruid of Wales, 1996-1999

The ecclesiastical parish of Llangiwg showing its administrative sub-divisions of Mawr, Blaenegel, Caegurwen and Alltygrug. Known as hamlets or districts in the historical record they were a common feature of many upland parishes in Wales. As sub-divisions of the parishes it was often they and not the parishes themselves which, from the sixteenth century, came to discharge the two basic aspects of local administration namely the relief of the poor and upkeep of the highways. At 12,550 acres Llangiwg was the second largest parish in the lordship of Gower only surpassed in size by Llangyfelach (27,305 acres). The greater part of the parish lay over 500 feet above sea level the highest points being Mynydd Alltygrug at Ystalyfera (1,173 feet), Penllerfedwen, overlooking Gwaun-Cae-Gurwen and Cwmgors (also 1,173 feet), Mynydd y Garth at Rhyd-y-fro (1,057 feet) and Cefn Gwrhyd (968 feet). It was bounded for the greater part by rivers: the Llynfell and Twrch, which rise in the Black Mountain, join near Gwys and take a south-easterly course to link up with the river Tawe at Ystalyfera. The Tawe then flows south west meeting the Upper Clydach river at Pontardawe. From the junction of these two rivers, the western boundary of the parish follows the course of the Upper Clydach to a point near Cwmgors, where it joins the river Gors. Finally, a part of the northern boundary follows the river Aman. Parochially, Llangiwg was bounded, in part, by Llangyfelach (and its administrative hamlet of Rhyndwyglydach), Cilybebyll (4,014 acres), Ystradgynlais (21,954 acres), Llanddeusant (10,307 acres), Llandeilo Fawr (25,628 acres) and Bettws (6,465 acres). A large part of the parish comprised common land notably on Gwauncaegurwen, Penllerfedwen, Garth, Gwrhyd and Mynydd Alltygrug. Although poor in fertility such land was important for game, building material, grazing and the exploitation of minerals. Indeed pasture and mineral rights were guarded vigilantly by the steward of the lord of Gower and transgressors punished. In 1801 the population of the parish was 829. In 1901 it was 12,376, such growth corresponding to expansion in local iron manufacture and the accompanying heavy demand for local coal. The most pronounced growth occurred in the district of Alltygrug which had a population of 197 in 1801 and 4,919 in 1861, this being primarily the result of iron manufactories at Ystalyfera and Ynyscedwyn.

Introduction

In 1910 Pontardawe was described in *Kelly's Directory of South Wales and Monmouthshire* as follows:

Pontardawe, a populous village, the greater portion of which is in Llanguicke,…is very prettily seated in the Swansea valley, $7\frac{1}{2}$ miles north-east from the town of Swansea and is the head of a (poor law) union formed in 1875 and also of a petty sessional division in the Western parliamentary division of Glamorgan and in the rural deanery of East Gower, archdeaconry of Carmarthen and diocese of St David's. The Swansea canal runs through and the Midland railway has a station here. The village is lighted by gas by the Pontardawe Gas Co. Limited. The church of St Peter (a chapel of ease to the parish church), erected in 1862, at a cost of about £10,000, is an edifice of Welsh sandstone, with Bath stone dressings, in the Gothic style, consisting of chancel, nave, aisles and an embattled western tower, 200 feet in height and containing one bell…The Public Hall and Institute, in Herbert Street, erected at a cost of £6,000 was opened in 1909. Here are steel, tinplate and chemical works. Alltycham, the residence of Ernest Hall Hedley esq JP occupies an eminence affording a delightful prospect. Brynheulog, the residence of Lewis Griffith Lewis esq is seated on a hill on the north-west side of the Swansea valley, with beautifully sloping grounds and commands views of nearly the whole length of the valley, as well as of the opposite side, and above the lovely dingle is Gellyonen mountain.

This second selection of images relating to Pontardawe and district includes several described in this passage. It follows closely the subject areas covered in volume one except that we have endeavoured to place greater emphasis on the outlying communities. There are also new features such as the chapters on the Lewises of Brynheulog and on the experiences of Pontardawe during wartime.

The great success of *Around Pontardawe* led to a very positive response to the appeal for material for a follow-up volume and we are very grateful to everyone who has contributed or offered help. This, one feels, is testimony to the perennial desire of the district's inhabitants to recapture and preserve the memories of its past. On the other hand, the social and physical transformations since the 1960s and the primary role played by Pontardawe today as a dormitory settlement for Swansea has meant that many members of the current generation are seemingly oblivious to the forces which fashioned the modern community. When one considers pre-Gilbertsonian Pontardawe the sense of temporal remoteness is even more acute, yet tangible reminders of this period abound – such as the canal and, of course, the farms, many of which date back 400 years or more. The ancient relics that litter the surrounding hills and which take us back to pre-history are another manifestation of the antiquity of the area.

Photographs can prove a rich historical legacy, one strongly illustrative of change. They can also rekindle our memories and stir our imagination in uniquely powerful and precious ways. The wide-ranging selection presented here is reflective of this, invoking as it does a tale of energy, enthusiasm, pathos and, on occasions, tragedy. Here can be found images of general scenes, standing structures, everyday lives, once in a lifetime occasions, work, recreation, schooldays and street life as well as the transport and industry of a now 'lost world'.

We hope that readers will enjoy this latest selection of photographs and also gain knowledge from the text which accompanies the images. While some people tend to think of history as something 'old', relating only to a distant past; urban development and social change, as well as being the hallmarks of contemporary history, are on-going dynamics which is why this volume includes some images from the 1980s.

In Pontardawe, the steelworks and coal industry have gone, as have the jobs they created. They have been replaced by industrial estates and supermarkets. Employment is now in modern factories set among green surroundings, a vast difference from the slag heaps and spoil tips of yesteryear. The district is facing the challenges of the post-industrial era with renewed confidence and, in this, the international music festival has played a catalytic role. Confidence is also apparent in the work of the Pontardawe Arts Centre, opened in 1996, which offers a wide variety of concerts and other events.

As we enter a new century and a new millennium it is fitting that this book should be dedicated to those who helped create and shape our community. Their perseverance and toil have given the present generation an interesting and socially rewarding place to live and work in – Pontardawe and district.

Note: The spellings of place-names in this compilation broadly accord with how they appeared in original documents and other sources. They do not necessarily reflect current written forms.

Taraful Soporul De Cimpe of Romania at the Pontardawe International Music Festival, 1993. 'The Festival', as it is known to the inhabitants of Pontardawe and district, has brought to the community a wealth of local, national and international culture in the forms of music, dance, song, costume, poetry and language. The festival has introduced musicians from as far afield as Russia, China, Australia, Senegal, Peru, Israel, Turkey, Hungary and Spain – to name but a few of the countries represented. Pontardawe people have been entertained by harp, hammered dulcimer, cymbalon, flute, kora, pan-pipes, charango, pibgorn, hurdy gurdy and sheng by groups and people with exotic sounding names such as Dembo Konte and Kausa Kuyateh, Dan ar Bras, Zi Lan Liao, Los Incas, Tarika, Guo Yue, Gregori Schechter and his Klezmer Festival Band. The festival, which began in 1977, is now a much respected international venue on the British music scene.

One
Maps and
General Scenes

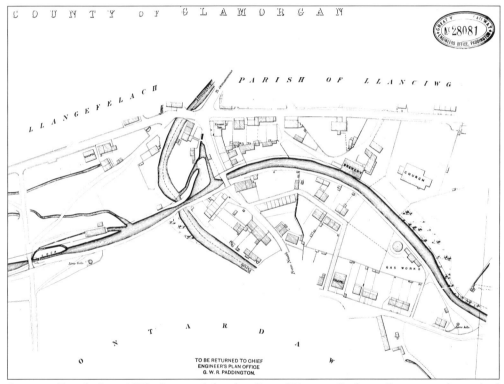

Swansea Canal plan, 1875. Surveyed for the Great Western Railway Company after it had purchased the canal in 1872, the plan highlights the development of Pontardawe around the waterway at that time. The growth of housing, service industries and light engineering is evident. Public houses, beer houses, inns, hotels, porter stores, chapels, churches, breweries, smiths, foundries, gasworks and a number of small terraces and courts all clustered into a small area to create the town of Pontardawe. The Cross Inn is marked at the crossroads with the town dock to the left of Herbert Street bridge. Barges would bring all manner of materials into the dock for use in the town and iron ore would be laden for shipment to the Ystalyfera iron works. The brewery is shown alongside the canal, as is the gasworks: both needed the canal for transporting commodities for their manufacturing processes. Adulum Baptist chapel which, with Horeb Welsh Wesleyan Methodist chapel, were the first non-conformist places of worship built in the emerging town (1845), had been joined in 1862 by the Anglican church of St Peter's. The growth of the town and the increase in population had created a demand for new religious establishments away from their traditional rural locations.

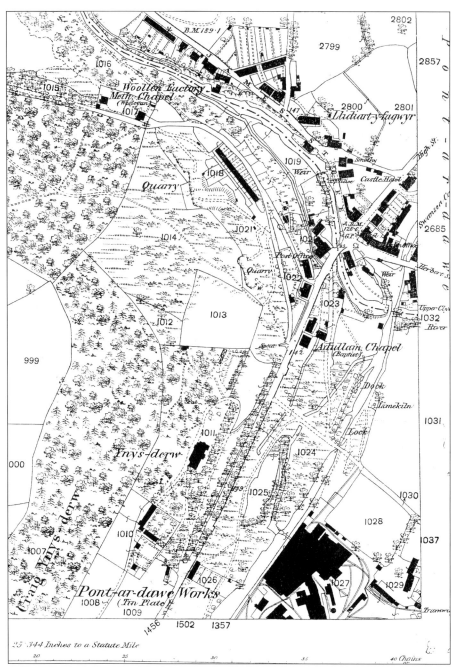

Pontardawe in 1877 showing the Maes Iago woollen factory (established pre-1851), the original Horeb Welsh Wesleyan Methodist chapel (built 1845), Primrose Row (built 1860), Llydiart y Fagwr (demolished *c.* 1900), Dynevor Arms (pre-1838), Victoria Inn (pre-1871), Castle Hotel (pre-1861), Cross Hotel (pre-1854), Dillwyn Arms (pre-1838), the town wharf (constructed *c.* 1797), the Cae'r Doc boat-building yard (established *c.* 1850), the former Cae'r Doc National School (established 1830), Carpenters Row (established *c.* 1830), Adulum Baptist chapel (built 1845), the works pond, the Pontardawe tinplate works, Ynysderw farmhouse and Ynysderw House (latter built *c.* 1855).

12

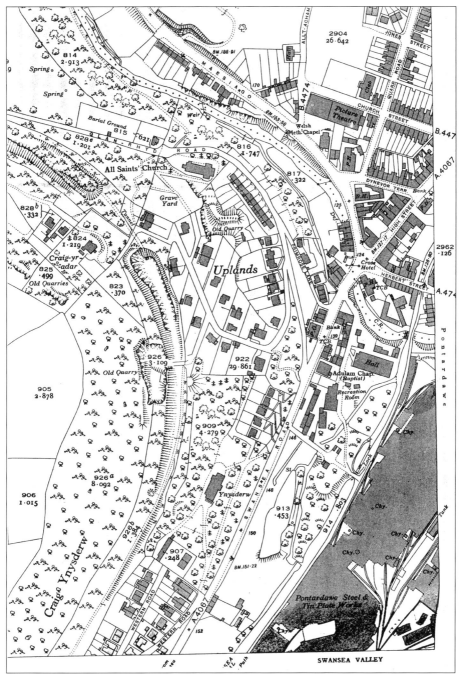

Pontardawe in 1942 showing urban development and the expansion of the Pontardawe steel and tinplate works (W. Gilbertson & Co. Ltd). Note the pre-1918 street developments (top right) on Dynevor Arms Land including Church Street and Dynevor Terrace (both pre-1898). The Pavilion cinema was licensed in 1914 while the Palais de Danse (later 'The Rink') was built before 1898 – both were originally skating rinks. The Uplands and Western Road are pre-1918 in origin while All Saints church opened in 1886. The aborted GWR line (constructed c. 1914) and 120 yard railway tunnel are also shown.

One of the earliest photographs of Pontardawe, *c.* 1880. This is in the vicinity of Cae'r Doc with, possibly, the former Cae'r Doc National School building to the left. St Peter's church towers imperiously in the distance. Also visible is the original humpback bridge over the canal, replaced in the 1930s. To its left, on Herbert Street, is London House, a draper's. Carpenters Row can be glimpsed to the right.

Pontardawe, *c.* 1905. In the immediate foreground is Brondeg House, built in 1862 as Ty Tyler by David Smith, land agent. This replaced a pre-1838 property and was later known as Gwynfryn. To its left are the towers of the Pontardawe chemical works. Beyond, lies Ynisderw Road (constructed from around 1895) and the first recreation ground of W. Gilbertson & Co. Carpenters Row can also be discerned as can most of the principal houses of the time, namely Gellygron, Brynheulog, Alltycham, Bryncelyn and Ynysygelynen.

This shows the area demarcated by High Street, Herbert Street, Holly Street and the Swansea Canal with the open fields of Ynysygelynen lying beyond, *c.* 1905. Soar Chapel is conspicuous while the cluster of buildings in the vicinity of the canal include, centre, the brewery (built, 1837/38) below which is the Co-operative building (1890) before it was extended in 1911 to accommodate a drapery store. Behind the Co-op were the timber yard and saw mills. The Foundry (1865) can be glimpsed, centre right, beyond Ynysygelynen bridge and the gasworks site (1869/70), without the gasometer, can be seen beyond the end of Orchard Street (pre-1877). The building with the stack is a blacksmith's shop. On the extreme right is the start of Carpenters Row, the white building being the Carpenters Arms which ceased trading in 1925/26.

Herbert Street, free of motor traffic, *c.* 1922. To the immediate left is the building premises of Ll. B. Williams. The latter lived at Pen-yr-Alltwen House and was instrumental in developing four quarries in that part of Alltwen. To the left, just past the bridge, lie blacksmith shops and beyond that the Pontardawe Inn (pre-1869). Opposite the latter is Midland House which, as Regent Buildings, housed J.D. Owen, draper, from 1923 to 1955. Note the arcade fronting the property which became the Continental Café in 1961.

The 'Tip' (above) and after reclamation (below), *c.* 1968 and *c.* 1975 respectively. The slag tip was pre-1918 in origin but grew extensively during the inter-war period covering most of the fields of the former Ynysderw Farm. The slag and other impurities were poured into the 'pit side' below the steelworks' furnaces where they solidified and were transferred by trucks to the slag site. Slag burners and derricks were situated on the tip which became a veritable lunar landscape. Many will no doubt recall the 'Sphinx-like' features that emerged such as those shown above and opposite. The three-storey properties in the centre are 60 and 62 Swansea Road, Trebanos. The remains of Graig Trebanos quarry can be seen in the background. Owned in 1910 by William Harries it had fine stone but was described at that time as a 'rough place'.

Another shot of the tip (above) and after seeding (below). The French firm Mouget and Co. Ltd worked the tip in 1962/63 extracting pure metal from the slag. The site was cleared from around 1972 and much of the area today is taken up by the new £10.5million Cwmtawe Comprehensive School and playing fields, all established on Parc Ynysderw, which was officially designated on 12 June 1979.

A fine view of part of the district from The Graig, Alltwen, 1937. The Glanrhyd tinplate works lies in the immediate foreground below Railway Terrace. The Imber factory has yet to be built. The 'rec' and secondary school playing fields lie to the left. Circumnavigating the latter is the railway track connecting the Glanrhyd tinplate works with the steelworks and the LMS railway. Note the marked bend in the river near the 'Cinders'. In the background looms Craig Llangiwg beneath which lie the workhouse and the start of Ynysmeudwy. Llwynmeudwy Isaf farm can be seen top centre right.

A later view of the district showing the Glanrhyd tinplate works and the Imber factory (left), c. 1953. The latter was built in 1952 on a three-acre site to house the Cambrian Dress Products Co. but the move never took place due to recession. The building was first occupied in 1954 by the Imber Research Company (incorporating Aladdin Industries Ltd) for the manufacture of oil heaters and lamps. It closed in 1980, the property subsequently being occupied by Matthews Building and Commercial Services Ltd (since 1981) while the remainder of the site currently serves as the Alltwen Industrial Estate, established in the early 1980s. The latter comprises eight units and is owned by the Welsh Development Agency, the land having been acquired by the Board of Trade in 1948. The house, left, is Craig yr Awel. Extreme centre left is Bryn Morgrug (historically Pant y Morgrug) which fell into ruin in the early 1960s and was subsequently demolished.

Two

Farms

Ynysderw Farm, *c.* 1925. The original farmhouse (right) and 'new' farmhouse survive miraculously in a sea of heavy industry, part of the W. Gilbertson & Co. complex. Both properties were demolished before the Second World War. Ynysderw covered 130 acres in 1838 when owned by the Cilybebyll estate. It was referred to as 'Enysddrow' in 1494/95 when owned by Morgan ap Ieuan ap David ap Oweyn. Along with Ynyspenllwch, Llachard Fawr and Alltyfanog it was one of the four 'ancient houses' of Rhyndwyglydach that belonged to the fourteenth-century bard and patriarch, Hywel Melyn. For many years the property was in the possession of Hywel's descendants, the Williams', having passed to Griffith Williams by 1650, son of William Griffith and Margaret, the daughter of Henry Penry of Alltyfanog. In the late seventeenth and early eighteenth centuries, Ynysderw was owned by another Griffith Williams whose wife Mary was the daughter of Richard Thomas (1631-1715) of Gellygron. Ynysderw came into the possession of the Herberts of Cilybebyll in 1710/11 and the land, together with the industrial complex, remained part of that estate until this century. Occupants of Ynysderw Farm included James Jervis (from 1744-70), David John (1770s), William Elias (1780s) and David Elias (1790s). John Jones (1776-1851) – 'Sion Ynysderw' – farmed the property between 1804 and 1851. He also had a brewery on the premises. His wife Hannah and five sons were named on the 1841 census enumerators' returns: Howell John; William; Llewellyn; Hopkin and John. Howell John was head of household in 1861. With him were his wife Margaret and their children: Hannah; Catherine; Jennett; John; Mary and Margaret. David Edwards was head of household in 1871 and 1881. The property was not named on the 1891 census.

Alltwen Ganol. This covered 58 acres in 1838 when owned by Howel Gwyn whose father William acquired it from the Briton Ferry estate in 1821. The site dates possibly from the fifteenth century as there is a reference to 'Alltewen' in 1493 though this may instead refer to Pen-yr-Alltwen Farm. The farm has been occupied by the Hopkins' since 1880, who bought the freehold from the Moore-Gwyn estate in 1925/26, though before this it was the abode of the ubiquitous Gibbs family. The property was bounded in 1838 by Alltwenchwith, Alltwen Uchaf and Cilhendre Fawr (incorporating Ty'n y Coedcae).

Ty'n y Cae, 1965. This covered 29 acres in 1838 when owned by Howel Gwyn and was previously part of the Briton Ferry estate. In that year it was known as Cwm y Llygod and was bounded by Alltwen Isaf, Alltwenchwith, Alltwen Common and Cilhendre Fawr. The farm was sold in 1972 for private housing development.

Cilhendre Fawr, *c.* 1960. This covered 256 acres in 1845, the largest farm in the district at that time. It lay in the ecclesiastical parish of Cadoxton juxta Neath and hamlet of Ynysymond and had formed part of the Briton Ferry estate until it was sold in 1821 to William Gwyn. The land is currently around 60 acres in area, much of it having been sold to the Forestry Commission. The Hopkins 'and Gibbs' were tenants in the nineteenth century while Ronnie James, undefeated British lightweight boxing champion 1944-47, came to live there in 1940. It was bounded in 1838 by Cilhendre Fach, Ynysymond Uchaf, Alltwen Isaf, Cwm y Llygod (Ty'n y Cae), Alltwenchwith, Alltwen Ganol, Alltwen Uchaf, Wernddu Uchaf and Craig yr Abbey. The earliest recorded reference is 'Kil yr Hendre' in 1584/85.

Penllwynteg. This covered 52 acres in 1838 when owned by the Cilybebyll estate. It was one of the oldest farmhouses in the area, there being a reference to 'Lloyn Tegey' in 1528. It was demolished in the 1980s. It was bounded in 1838 by Gellinudd Arms and Lands, Keeper's Lodge (Cilybebyll Fach), Maes Llan and Tir Dan yr Eglwys.

Gwrach-y-llwynau Farm, Trebanos, c. 1950. This covered 15 acres in 1838 when part of the Miers estate centred on Ynyspenllwch and was bounded by Graig Trebanos, Gellyonen Ganol and Ty'n y Coed Isaf. The main dwelling consisted of a kitchen, parlour, dairy, pantry and three bedrooms while the outbuildings comprised a cow-house, stable (once used as a carpenter's shop), cart-house, barn and two pigsties. The house behind is Highmead. Heol y Llwynau, Farm Road and Heol y Ffin lie on the land today. The farmhouse was demolished in the 1950s and the Trebanos housing estate, built on Gwrach-y-llwynau land, opened in March 1963.

Graig Trebanos Farm shortly before its demolition in 1959 showing, as insert, Mrs Mary Jones, its last inhabitant. It stood at the junction of Pheasant Road with New Road and had been ruined for some years. It had thick walls while its roof was partly thatched and partly covered with stone. It was replaced with two council houses. It was one of two Graig Trebanos farms in the area, the other becoming known, successively, as Graig Trebanos Cottage, Trebanos House and (currently) St Bernard's Nursing Home. The farm above covered 61 acres in 1838 and formed part of the Ynyspenllwch estate. It was bounded in that year by Gwrach-y-llwynau, Gellyonen Ganol, Gellyonen Uchaf, Gwybedin (or Penygraig) and Graig Trebanos.

Penygraig, 1924. Historically it was known as Gwybedin ('gnat', 'insect', 'mosquito'), Bwlch y Gwybedin lying below the farm. It covered 57 acres in 1838 when owned by Thomas Lott Martin, eldest son of Edward and Martha Martin of Ynystawe, though hitherto it had been in the direct ownership of the Duke of Beaufort. It later formed part of the Miers' Ynyspenllwch estate. In 1838 it was bounded by Mynydd Gellyonen, Plasnewydd, Gellyonen Uchaf, Graig Trebanos and the Graig Trebanos sheepwalk. There is a superb vista of the Upper Swansea valley from Penygraig.

Ynysmeudwy Isaf. This covered 93 acres in 1838 when owned by Howell Williams, though it had previously formed part of the Ynyscedwyn estate. It was bounded in that year by Ynysygelynen, Tir y Bont, Alltycham, Ynysmeudwy Ganol, Pant y Morgrug and Glyndolau. The latter two were in Cilybebyll parish, Ynysmeudwy Isaf at one time owning the land on which the Glantawe tinplate works was established (1879). The farm is currently up for sale.

Hay making on Ynysmeudwy Uchaf farm, 1933, showing the then owner, Hopkin John who was reputedly the last farmer to use oxen-drawn equipment in the Swansea valley. The farm comprised 170 acres in 1838 when owned by Edward Thomas Thomas of the Glanmor estate, Swansea. Before 1821 it had been part of the Briton Ferry estate. The farm was bounded in 1838 by Ynysmeudwy Ganol, Gellyfowy Ganol, Gellyfowy Fawr and Cilmaengwyn Isaf. The Ynysmeudwy Arms incorporates the original farmhouse, the new farmhouse lying next to the public house. On part of Ynysmeudwy Uchaf are the remains of a branch canal, constructed in 1828, which connected the Swansea Canal with the Waunycoed Colliery.

Gellyfowy Fawr. This covered 222 acres in 1838 when part of the Ynyscedwyn estate. In 1650 Charles Awbrey was occupier of 'Gellyvowis mawr'. In the second half of the nineteenth century it was the abode of Thomas Lott Martin. The property was bounded in 1838 by Gellyfowy Fach, Gellyfowy Ganol, Pantgwyn, Ynysmeudwy Uchaf, Ynysmeudwy Ganol, Cilmaengwyn Ganol, Cilmaengwyn Isaf, Ty'n y Coed and Cwmnantllicky. The farmhouse has been derelict since the 1960s.

Three
Transport

Swansea Canal at Pontardawe. This superb scene was captured by David Williams of Pontardawe Grammar School around 1960, depicting the canal flowing close to where the leisure centre stands today. In the foreground is lock number 10 (Ynysderw Lock) with the lock pound beyond. The sites of the old sheet mills and billet mill of the steelworks are on the right hand side of the towpath. Lock number 11 (Works Lock) can be seen alongside the 180 foot high chimney stack of the former billet mill boiler house. It is to be regretted that Pontardawe lost so much of its heritage and beauty when this section of canal was infilled around 1970.

Ynysygelynen bridge, Pontardawe, c. 1965. Also known as Holly Street bridge to local residents, it was constructed in 1796 to allow horse and pedestrian traffic to cross the newly completed Swansea Canal. The bridge was typical of the over-bridges erected by the canal company at that time. This old stone bridge was removed in 1966 and replaced by a concrete slab structure, the reason being that buses of that period were having difficulty crossing the humpback bridge and were frequently grounded in the centre.

Lengthman's hut, Ynysmeudwy. Constructed by the Swansea Canal Navigation Company in 1826 as a 'residence' for the lock-keeper who operated the two locks at Ynysmeudwy, the dwelling was built on the island formed by the lock chamber and the bypass channel which allowed surplus water to bypass the lock. Externally, the residence was only 13 feet 7 inches long by 10 feet 5 inches wide. Internal measurements were 9 feet by 7 feet 6 inches. The internal features comprised a hearth and four stone recesses which were used as cupboards. The building was restored by the Swansea Canal Society between 1985 and 1986.

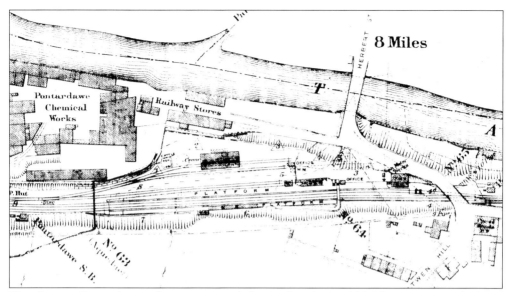

Plan showing Pontardawe railway station and chemical works, *c.* 1925. There were two platforms at the station with (from 1860) regular passenger and goods services up and down the valley. The station acted as a goods depot for the area with sidings and storage sheds constructed for the reception and despatch of goods and other materials. Passenger services ceased in 1950 and the freight line closed in 1964. The chemical works was erected in 1851 and was one of the major industries in Pontardawe producing vitriol and sulphuric acid for various tinplate works in the area. It closed in 1931 as a result of an agreement of December 1930 which saw it and five similar South Wales establishments acquired by the National Smelting Company who required them to cease manufacture and commence demolition of their plants by 1 January 1932.

Goods and coal yards located behind the 'up' platform of Pontardawe station, *c.* 1920. Also shown is Chemical Road leading to the chemical works in the immediate foreground. The slate-roofed building (just visible centre, bottom) is, or became, 'Min-yr-Afon' and was located on the site of the Pontardawe flour mill, whose remnants may be below the chemical works tower. The large building, centre, was used as a biscuit depot in the early 1960s. Nearly all the buildings around the station and chemical works have been demolished and replaced with a new road network (the A4067) and bridges serving Pontardawe and the Swansea valley.

Primrose Colliery tramroad. It was constructed around 1820 to haul coal from John Parsons' mines in Rhos to a wharf on a private branch canal built in 1825/26 which connected to the Swansea Canal. It came into the ownership of the Primrose Colliery Company after 1840. Early horse-drawn railways such as the Primrose were referred to as 'tramroads' or 'dramroads' in Wales. The tramroad was narrow gauge of approximately 24 inches between the rails and used horses and winches as motive power to move the drams. The bridge seen here was constructed in 1859/60 to enable the tramroad to continue working over the newly built Swansea Vale Railway. The tramroad ceased working before 1913 but was re-opened by the Ynysfechan Colliery which lay directly below the bridge to the left and closed in 1927.

An evocative 1952 shot of the LMS line at Pontardawe at the junction with the branch line to Pontardawe steelworks. The latter was originally a pre-1878 tramway which was converted into a railway by 1898. Note the busy traffic at the intersection. The trucks of the branch line are crossing the small wooden bridge that passed over the road to the 'Sychan' (a contraction of Ynysfechan). The large wooden bridge that crossed the river Tawe lay a little further on. Both bridges were demolished around 1973. The administrative offices of Richard Thomas and Baldwins Ltd can be seen in the background as can the steelworks' canteen, the sheetworks and the former buildings of the chemical works that had been closed for twenty years.

Pontardawe railway station, 1923. Celebration of the creation of the London, Midland and Scottish Railway Company (LMS). The station originally served the Swansea Vale Railway, from 1860 to 1876 when the Midland Railway Company purchased the line. Note the wonderful variety of headgear.

Railway crossing gates, Herbert Street, 1970. The gates served a branch line which started in the vicinity of the Carpenter's Shop of the steelworks (later the site of the Swansea Valley Ventilation Co. Ltd or the 'Sheet and Metal') and ran parallel to the river Tawe (on the works' side) as far as the Glanrhyd tinplate works. The line, which closed in 1962, also served Pontardawe sheetworks. The building just visible on the left is the Continental Café which closed in 1968. In the distance lie Tanyrallt House and Mill Row.

Alltwen Isaf railway viaduct, 1987. A well remembered feature in this part of Alltwen close to the historic boundary between the ecclesiastical parishes of Cilybebyll and Cadoxton juxta Neath, delineated by the Nant Llechau (seen here). The viaduct was constructed in 1860 and demolished in 1988 as part of the construction works for Phase 2 of the A4067, which opened on 20 December 1988. The tunnel and embankment lay on Alltwen Isaf land. The Nant Llechau bridge, right, gave access to the Llechau smallholding and was subsequently rebuilt.

The premier mode of transport at one time – the ubiquitous horse and cart, c. 1923. This one is outside Albert Hardy's metal merchant's business, 22 High Street, Pontardawe. In more recent times the premises became a Labour Exchange. The keen-eyed will notice 'The Palace' poster in the window. The Palace later became the Lyric cinema (see p. 70). The steps lead to 26 High Street.

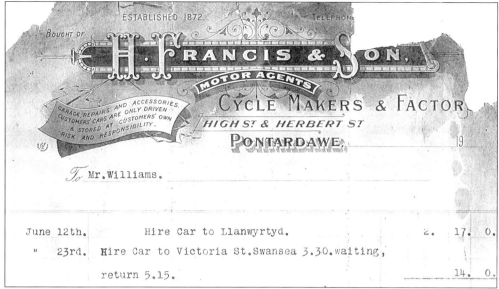

H. Francis and Son ('Franson') letterhead, dated 27 June 1917. The business was established as a transport concern in Herbert Street in 1872. By 1917 the business had two premises manufacturing cycles and also operating as a motor factor, hiring out vehicles. The hire charges are interesting: to hire a car and driver from Pontardawe to Swansea and return, including waiting time, the princely sum of 14s was charged.

A 'Franson' twenty-seat charabanc, in 1908. Typical of the Edwardian era was the trip by charabanc for local associations. The make of vehicle is unknown, as is its location, but of interest is the chain drive on the rear wheels, the iron wheels with solid rubber tyres, the handbrake outside the body, paraffin lamps and the large horn. After serving the community for many years the vehicle eventually ended up in Mr Greggor Oates' motors in Nairobi where it was recorded in 1954.

Lewis Bros charabancs in Grove Road, with the manse of Tabernacle chapel in the background, c. 1915. The vehicles were probably a Dodge and an Albion and were used as hire vehicles or taxis by Lewis Bros' various business enterprises including mineral water, coal and the Palais de Danse (later 'The Rink') which they owned. The vehicle parked nearest the manse doubled as a delivery vehicle for the mineral water produced at the Grove Road factory. Note the solid rubber tyres and the open nature of the driver's and passengers' compartments.

'The Lark' omnibus, c. 1925. The vehicle was on a trip from Pontardawe to the Capitol Cinema, Ystalyfera, the latter having opened on August Bank Holiday, 1924. The advertisement reads: 'Capitol Cinema For Pictures, Music & Comfort'. The gentleman standing to the right is Les Davies, whose father owned the firm, one of many private haulage companies operating in south Wales. Again, note the solid rubber tyres along with the headlamps, mud guards and the 'steep-sided' passenger compartment, the latter typical of the period.

Four
Iron, Steel and Tinplate

W. Gilbertson & Co., *c.* 1925. Fields formerly belonging to Ynysderw Farm had been completely covered by industrial buildings. Centre left, from left to right, lie the billet mill, bar mill, casting pit and melting shop. The electric shop is in the centre. The original tinplate works and old sheet mills lie centre bottom. Remarkably the 'old' and 'new' Ynysderw farmhouses still survive behind the assorting room of the new tinplate works. Opposite the assorting room stands the slag, manure and cement works. The sheetworks lies in the distance next to the undeveloped Ynysygelynen fields. Bottom left is the former smallholding that abutted The Avenue, owned by William Williams, 'Corn Stores'. The steelworks closed in September 1962 and the area lay derelict for a decade or so. The stacks were demolished around 1965 and this stretch of the Swansea Canal was drained around 1970. Most of the plant was demolished and the site cleared by 1973, the principal exceptions being: the former tinplate works buildings; the electric shop; the general stores; the administrative offices and the steelworks canteen. After Parc Ynysderw was designated in 1979 the site underwent a range of modern developments, including Pontardawe RFC Clubhouse (opened 1979), the leisure centre (opened 1985), and Gateway's supermarket (opened 1986 – Somerfield's since 1994).

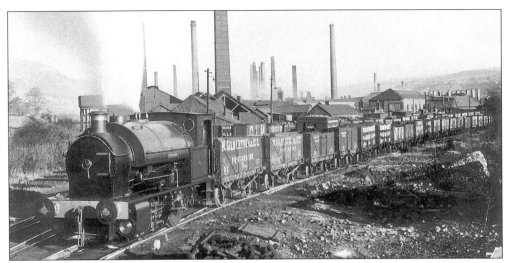

Pontardawe steel and tinplate works (W. Gilbertson & Co.), *c.* 1932. The steelworks had its own internal railway, fleet of locomotives and rolling stock. The railway system was used for transporting iron, steel, tinplate, scrap metal, coal and slag waste in the main works as well as between the secondary establishments of the Gilbertson 'empire' at Glanrhyd and the sheetworks. This scene shows the locomotive *Pontardawe* pulling a fleet of Gilbertson wagons containing coal. *Pontardawe* was a saddle tank locomotive built in 1932 by Beyer Peacock and Company of Gorton, Manchester. The locomotive looks in pristine condition and one suspects that the photograph was taken when the engine was delivered new in 1932. The tinplate departments are to the right of the single tall chimney and the steel-making ones to the left.

Pontardawe steelworks and Swansea Canal, seen from the Herbert Street canal bridge looking south towards the then closed steelworks, 1965. The buildings alongside the canal consisted primarily of the former bar mill, billet mill and melting shop. The chimneys on the left are the four melting shop boiler stacks, the tinplate boiler house stack (180 feet high) and the old sheet mill boiler stack. The chimney near the canal is the former billet mill boiler house stack with the reheating furnace stack beyond. The end house of Carpenters Row (No. 6) is visible to the left, which had formerly been occupied by George Holloway and his family. The building on the right is Ellis' the drapers, lately the Canal Restaurant. The Upper Clydach aqueduct on the canal can be identified by the stone wall where the canal narrows.

The interior of Pontardawe steelworks, showing a ladle full of molten steel about to be poured into ingot moulds in the casting pit below, c. 1950. Most of the steel produced at Pontardawe was obtained from scrap metal which was brought to the works via the LMS and branch railways. A crane loaded the scrap into a 'charger' which then placed the scrap in the furnace. The original open-hearth furnaces established in 1890 were coal-fired but these were later changed to gas, oxygen being blown in to provide rapid combustion. The works closed in September 1962 and the site of the casting pits is today occupied by a Somerfield supermarket.

Munition workers at W. Gilbertson & Co., Pontardawe, during the First World War. Pig iron marked 'Trent' had been brought to the Pontardawe steelworks from the Trent Iron Company in Lincolnshire to be mixed or blended with Gilbertson's iron to produce a steel suitable for munitions. The steel would be rolled into round bars which were then delivered to the munition factories for the production of shells. Large numbers of men volunteered to fight in the armed forces (278 from Gilbertson's alone during the First World War) resulting in a shortage of labour in the heavy industries which necessitated the employment of women. Annie Davies (Penparc, Rhos) is at bottom right, with Jack Williams top left.

W. Gilbertson & Co.'s ambulance team, at Gellygron House, home of Charles G. Gilbertson, in 1928. Pictured are the committee and administrators of the first ambulance purchased by the company, reflecting the philanthropic nature of the Gilbertson family at this time. On the left, George Smith (trustee) and W.A. Madge (first aid department) stand in front of the vehicle with Phillip Humphries (driver) kneeling. At the far right are Mark James (benevolent fund secretary), James Bevan (vice chairman of the committee) with D.T. Duncan (book holder) kneeling. From left to right, back row, sitting: Captain G.W.A. Doe (chairman and welfare supervisor), G.M. Harry (secretary), Charles G. Gilbertson JP and county councillor, Ben Thomas (trustee) and W. Pugh (treasurer). Front row: D.J. Jones (hospital representative), D.S. Thomas (book holder), Alf Evans (book holder) and Isaac Powell (book holder).

Administrative staff, Richard Thomas and Baldwins Ltd, Pontardawe, 1962. From left to right, back row: David Thomas Davies, Sid Williams, Len Hodgkish, David Clee, Alan John, Selwyn Lloyd. Third row: Jack Rogers, Brynmor Davies, Lavinia Jones, Evelyn Roberts, Maldwyn Richards. Second row: Winnie Hudson, David Howel James, Tom Davies, Tom Canning (steelworks manager), Gwen Pugh, Emrys Davies. Front: Elunud Barratt, Glyn Rees, Ros Bodycombe, Viv Morgan and Rita Edwards.

Pickling department, Pontardawe tinplate works, c. 1950. This scene shows the semi-automated process in use at that time. Prior to this the 'dippers' would have had to dip each plate individually by hand. Iron cradles carry stacks of black plate from the cold rolls department to the pickling department for cleaning. The pickling consisted of dipping the black plate (un-tinned) into vats of sulphuric acid diluted to 5% acid with water. The acid removed mill scale, grease, dirt and any foreign material from the surface of the steel plates prior to the next process – tinning. The fumes visible in the air contained steam and acid, all part of the normal working environment. Health and safety were not important considerations for the work force at that time.

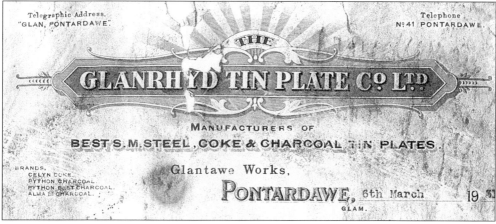

Glanrhyd Tinplate Company Limited, 1931. Known to those who worked there as the Glantawe works as it was originally the Glantawe Tinplate Company in 1879 but was acquired by W. Gilbertson & Co. in 1883 and re-registered as the Glanrhyd Tinplate Company. The letterhead advertises 'Best S.M. Steel, Coke and Charcoal Tin Plates.' The S.M. steel was mild steel produced by the Siemens-Martin open-hearth process which was the method of production at the Pontardawe steelworks from 1890 to 1962. Coke and charcoal tin plates were steel plates manufactured from iron using coke or charcoal as a fuel and deemed to be free from impurities such as sulphur which coal was liable to introduce into the iron or steel. Tinplate from the Glanrhyd works was exported to Canada for the packing of salmon.

The (former) Bryn tinplate works, Ynysmeudwy, 1949. This view shows the typical external buildings of a south Wales tinplate works. Depicted is a bank of furnaces with one chimney serving a pair of furnaces. The latter enabled the furnaceman to keep each pair of mills supplied with sufficient quantities of hot sheets for rolling by the mill teams. The works closed in 1941 and its equipment was removed for scrap.

Bryn tinplate works hot mill team, 1924. There were four hot mills at the Bryn works each with its own team of mill men and women. This team consisted of, from left to right, back row: Will Jones, Tom Morgan, Bill James. Front: Anthony Joseph, Margaret Landry, Bob Williams, Bill Joseph. Margaret is holding the tin slasher's knife which was used to open or force apart the packs of sheets which had become stuck together under the pressure of the rolls. After opening, the sheets passed from the hot mill to the annealing department, then through the pickling, cold rolls, tinning and assorting departments. The brands of tinplate produced at the Bryn works were 'Cennen', 'Carnedd', 'Best', 'Illtyd', 'Brython', 'Millbrook' and 'Aber'.

Five
Other Industries

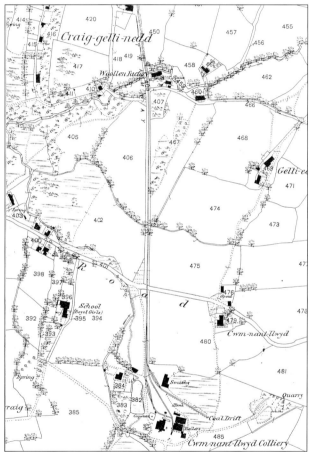

Map of Gellinudd and district, 1878. Centre is the tramway connecting the Waunycoed and Cwmnantllwyd collieries (latter shown bottom). Both were constituent parts of The South Wales Primrose Coal Company Ltd. The mines were connected to the Swansea Canal by a timber trestle bridge which crossed the river Tawe and connected with a branch of the main canal. At Waunycoed was an incline which led to Cwmnantllwyd at the top of which was a large drum which enabled a cable attached to the full descending drams to pass around the drum and pull up empty drams. Also shown is the Gellinudd Board School, built on Ty'n y Graig (Ganol) land, which opened in 1874 and closed in 1903. The woollen factory was powered by the Nant Gellinudd and was owned by Jacob Thomas in 1871. It fell into disuse later that decade. Cwmnantllwyd and Gelligeiros farms were part of the Cilybebyll estate until 1957. Extreme top left, centre, is the Gellinudd Arms, an abode of some notoriety which closed in 1927.

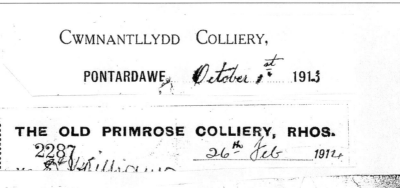

Cwmnantllydd Colliery,

Pontardawe, *October 1st* 1913

THE OLD PRIMROSE COLLIERY, RHOS.

2287 *St Williams* *26th Feb* 1914

The South Wales Primrose Coal Co., Ld. No. 839

THE TARENI COLLIERY COY. LTD.

PONTARDAWE, *7th Nov* 1929

Letterheads depicting collieries of yesteryear: the South Wales Primrose Coal Company Ltd, 1929 (revealing that the Tareni Colliery Company Ltd was a separate entity at that time); the Old Primrose Colliery, Rhos (1914) and the Cwmnantllydd (*sic* Cwmnantllwyd) Colliery (1913). The Old Primrose opened in 1840 and closed pre-1918. Seams and levels of the Cwmnantllwyd colliery closed in 1908, 1910, 1911, 1914, 1924, 1927, 1928 and 1944 (those for Waunycoed in 1907, 1910, 1916, 1920 and 1964).

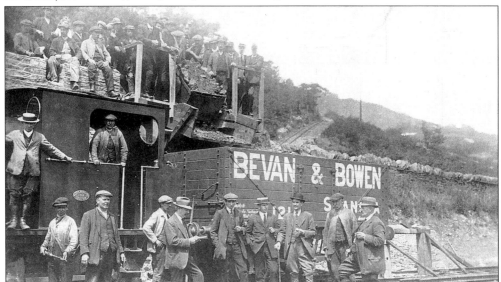

(Re-)opening of the Graig Colliery, Trebanos, July 1916. This was the Daren Colliery owned by the Graig Colliery Company which had been formed around 1904 (the 'Graig' may denote Graig Trebanos on whose land the colliery lay). The Great Western Railway reached Trebanos from Clydach in 1915 and the colliery was re-opened in 1916 to take advantage of it. The locomotive pictured was built in Leeds in 1908 by Manning, Wardle & Co. 'Bevan and Bowen', emblazoned on the coal trucks, were coal proprietors, who owned the Upper Graigola Colliery, Glais and whose registered office was 10 Somerset Place, Swansea.

Pithead baths (foreground) and screens (right) at the Daren Colliery, Trebanas. The colliery closed in 1964, this photograph being taken shortly afterwards. The baths were subsequently converted into the Trebanos RFC clubhouse (opened 1968). Note the disused coal trams. The area where the railway runs was subsequently cleared.

Daren Colliery, pay hut, 1964. Receiving their last pay packets are, from left to right: Dan Turner (Craigcefnparc), Brian Davies ('Frankie') and John Jenkins. So ended a tradition of coal mining on Graig Trebanos which dated back several centuries. An anonymous contemporary account written by a former miner stated: 'There was nothing modern in the working of coal at the Daren. The colliers worked the coal with picks but did a fair amount of blasting the coal loose with explosives. It was then filled by shovel into trams. The trams were drawn two or three at a time by ponies to the main haulage junctions where a journey of sixteen to eighteen trams was made by connecting them with shackles. The trams were then sent out of the mine by a steel rope worked off a haulage engine. Even though Daren was an old-fashioned colliery it had a very high production rate. There was (also) a friendly atmosphere at the colliery not met with in the large modern mines.'

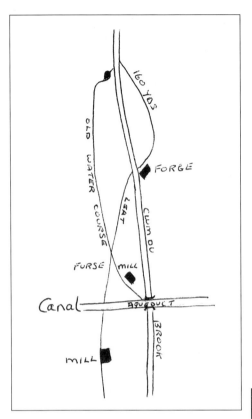

Ynysmeudwy. This early Briton Ferry estate plan, dated *c.* 1820, shows industries that existed at Ynysmeudwy prior to the establishment of the Ynysmeudwy brickworks and pottery in 1845. The plan shows the Swansea Canal which had been completed to this location by 1796 and the Cwmdu aqueduct which carried the canal over the Cwmdu stream. The plan was drawn to highlight watercourses on the stream which were using water to power waterwheels in the industries shown. An 'old water leat' carried water to a furze mill near the aqueduct (which would have been used to crush gorse for use as animal feed). A water leat, 160 yards long, carried water to a forge and a third leat took water into Ynysmeudwy corn mill. The latter lay on the Briton Ferry estate owned by the Mansel family and had ceased to function after 1796 due to the canal severing its water supply. William Thomas occupied the mill in 1677; Charles Williams in 1693 and Thomas Walter Plumer in 1700.

Screens at Cwmnant colliery, Ynysmeudwy, 1983. This scene shows surface workings of a small mine, typical of the industry during the 1970-90 period and very different from the large deep mines with their winding towers and pithead gear. The screens sorted the coal into various sizes. A chute is visible on the right-hand side for loading the coal into lorries. Behind the screens was a winding engine, a diesel winch which was used to haul the drams out of the mine to the surface. Cwmnant colliery operated from 1977 to 1982 working the Upper Pinchin coal seam and producing steam coal for use by power stations.

A view of the 160 foot tower structures that housed the winding gear for the upcast and downcast shafts at Abernant colliery, just prior to their demolition on 10 June 1989 following the colliery's closure in 1988. The surface was cut in 1952 with production starting in 1956. The colliery, which was a National Coal Board showpiece, opened in order to mine the rich seams of anthracite coal in the Peacock and Red Veins. However, the difficulties encountered in mining the former, meant only the Red Vein could be worked economically. The opening of the Bettws drift mine and the devastating effect of the 1984/85 miners' strike, coupled with government policy not predisposed to coal as a major fuel, proved to be the death knell for the colliery.

Building workers for Williams Bros, Building and Civil Engineering Contractors, Pontardawe, c. 1935. The workers were engaged in building a flood protection wall along the river Tawe close to where the Pontardawe Leisure Centre now stands. The persons identified are, from left to right, second row: Llewelyn Williams (fourth), D.R. Williams (sixth), Haydn Williams (eighth), John Hywel Roberts (ninth). Front, third from left, is William John Williams. At the back is 'Chips', who could lift two cwt. bags of cement on the end of a shovel. The business was established in 1890 by the five sons of Rees Williams: John, Llewelyn, Ivor, William and Dan; John Rees buying his brothers out around 1912. David Rees, John's son, became a partner in the 1930s while Haydn, another of John's sons, was a partner during the Second World War to 1951 when he left and was replaced by Gordon, David's son. At its peak the firm employed 300 people. The business was located for most of its life where the Avenue Garage now stands only moving to the Thomas Street site in 1957. It ceased operations in December 1983.

Quarry at Alltycham woods, Pontardawe, 1911. There have been many quarries operating around Pontardawe notably in Trebanos, Alltwen and Ynysmeudwy. Alltycham quarries consisted of a number of workings on the upper reaches of Barley Hill. This particular quarry was opened to supply building stone for the construction of the Pontardawe Higher Elementary School (opened in 1913), later the grammar school. The stone worked was Pennant Sandstone, a hard-wearing durable material very suited to the atmosphere in south Wales which suffered greatly from air-borne pollution. Notice the heavy sledgehammers and large steel chisels which were used to break the stone.

Construction of the Berlei (UK) Ltd factory, 1964. Originally (1961) based at 'The Rink', it opened on this new site, previously occupied by the Pavilion cinema, in September 1964 and employed 200. It manufactured ladies' foundation garments, specialising in corsetry and brassieres. Berlei's ceased production in 1982, Morris Cohen Ltd taking over operations that year. In 1995 Bairdwear Ltd replaced Morris Cohen as owners but have recently announced the factory's closure.

Qualiton Records (Wales) Ltd established a site in Pontardawe at Works Lane in 1958 under three directors: John Edwards, Douglas Rosser and Mrs O. Edwards, though the company had been processing gramophone records in London since at least January 1957. The company moved to a new factory in December 1964, the former steel and tinplate works' canteen, Ynisderw Road. It subsequently traded as Qualiton Records (1968) Ltd and was acquired by Decca Records in that year, who almost immediately closed the premises down, transferring operations to their New Malden, Surrey, site.

Ruined buildings of the Economic Hot Water Supply Company Ltd at the 'Sychan', 1987. The company was established in 1948 by Wilfred Morgan and Wilfred Evans of the Pontardawe Coal and Metals and Engineering Company, founded around 1928. The P.C.M.E.C. owned the 'Sychan' site which lay on Gwyn's Drift Yard and had been a scrapyard in the 1930s. The E.H.W.S.C.L.'s 'Sychan' premises replaced the former factory at Ynisderw Road (now Neuadd Henoed). Operations were transferred from the 'Sychan' to the Pontardawe tinplate works buildings in 1958. The E.H.W.S.C.L. manufactured copper cylinders and back boilers for domestic usage (making use of the 'Owen's Patent'). Its successors, from 1959, still occupy the tinplate works site today. The 'Sychan' buildings were demolished around 1990.

Pontardawe Timber Supplies, Chemical Road, 1987. The building was originally railway stores for the LMS railway (see map on p. 27). In the early 1960s the manufacture of belts took place there while BAW Engineering, makers of specialised tools, was a subsequent occupier of the site. Pontardawe Timber Supplies was the final business there, the premises being the last to be demolished in the road following the construction of Phase 2 of the A4067 in 1988.

Old blacksmith's shop, Rhyd-y-fro, *c.* 1925. The blacksmith made and repaired all types of agricultural machinery and implements as well as household items. Note the newly made hay rakes and repaired grass cutting machine with its blades protected by timber. Shovel blades are hanging on the open door. Included in the photograph are, from left to right: Tom Williams (blacksmith), John Evan Jenkins (farrier), Dan Morgan (miller at Gellygron corn mill) and Mr Williams of Trebanos (wheelwright). The site is today occupied by A & M Taxis and used as a repair garage.

Gellygron corn and flour mill, *c.* 1930. The mill was an integral part of the rural community and the Rhyd-y-fro area, processing corn and grain supplied not only from local farms but also from places further afield. The mill was built on the western bank of the Upper Clydach river and was powered by an overshot water wheel. The water was brought to the mill via a race to a large storage pond directly above the mill buildings; it then passed through a sluice gate to provide power to drive the wheel. This mill was one of a series located on the Upper Clydach river at Rhyd-y-fro, the others being Felin Uchaf, now a private property and the woollen mill located below the Royal Oak public house. Today, Gellygron mill lies in ruins.

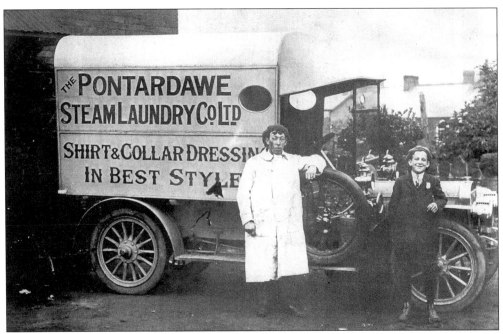

Pontardawe Steam Laundry Company Limited. The business was established in 1904 at 3 Fuller Street Pontardawe, John Spencer taking out the lease for the property and business from 29 September that year. He was presumably involved in the business. The two photographs show the progression from horse-drawn vehicles in 1904 to motorised transport around 1910. Laundry companies were an important element in any community before the advent of gas and electric irons. The only other available ironing aid to the housewife at this time was the heavy smoothing iron which had to be heated in front of an open fire.

Pontardawe gasworks, *c.* 1985. The Pontardawe Gas Company was established in 1869/70 adjacent to the Swansea Canal. At that time nearly every town had its own gas company supplying the immediate district with town gas produced from coal. The coal was brought to the gasworks at Pontardawe by canal barge. A new gasworks was erected on the site after 1910 with the addition of a large gasometer near The Foundry. The gasometer shown was the third tank constructed at the canal-side depot and was decommissioned around 1987. The buildings in the foreground were the former Pontardawe Rural District Council's highways depot. Cae'r Pandy park now occupies most of the site, opened in 1988.

Gas share certificate, 1873, bought by Philip Morgan of Heol Ddu and Alltyfanog farms. An Extraordinary General Meeting for the winding up of the Pontardawe Gas Company, on account of its liabilities, took place at the Cross Inn Hotel in August 1891, the notice of the meeting being signed by David Smith (land agent), John Morgan (surveyor) and Robert Evans (iron founder, 'The Foundry'). Ownership later became vested, variously, in the Bryncelyn Gas Company, The Tawe Valley Gas Company and the Pontardawe Gas Undertaking.

Lewis Bros Mineral Water Works, Pontardawe. The most important ingredient of mineral water or 'pop', was the syrup. The process of making syrup was by mixing the various essences (highly concentrated fruit juices), flavours and sweeteners into a very concentrated liquid. A small quantity of the prepared syrup would then be fed into each pop bottle with water and carbonated gas added to make up the correct volume. The photograph shows bottles of fruit essences and foaming liquid in the syrup room. Note the 'Rodine', a rat and mouse poison.

A sample of Lewis' pop bottle labels. Those displayed were in production around 1930.

Six

The Lewises of Brynheulog

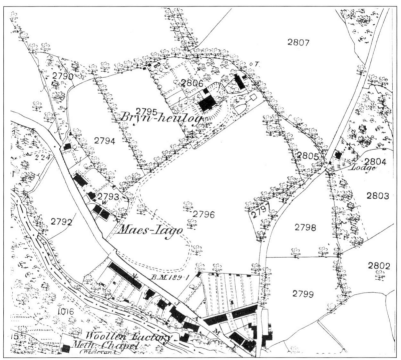

Brynheulog, 1877. The land originally formed part of Maes Iago, 11 acres being conveyed from Phillip Williams, master weaver, to Jacob Lewis, chemical manufacturer on 18 November 1858. The next day, three acres were given by Jacob Lewis to his son Lewis Griffith including a messuage (i.e. Brynheulog) 'in the course of construction'. In 1873 Lewis was conveyed a further 10 acres by his mother. In 1896 the property was valued at £3,390 and comprised: a basement with 'two good cellars'; a ground floor with dining room, drawing room, library, china pantry, and a first floor which had five bedrooms and a bathroom with hot and cold supply. A cow house, stable, harness room and chaff room with two coach houses stood in the yard. The house stood on an elevation commanding extensive views with a lawn tennis court and garden adjoining. In addition it was 'fairly well supplied with water' from a well sunk down to the rock from which it was believed a 'never failing supply' was available. Brynheulog was positioned with a view across the valley to the Pontardawe chemical works and it was said that Lewis Griffith Lewis could tell from the colour of the smoke coming from the factory chimney if there was a problem which needed his attention! The house remained a family home for three generations before it was demolished in 1978/79. The lodge, shown to the right (and still extant), served Alltycham House.

Ynysygelynen, centre left, *c.* 1905. Referred to as 'Enys Kylenen' in 1504 when a grant was made by David ap John ap David to Griffith ap John ap Griffith. It came into the ownership of the Cilybebyll estate in 1710/11 and was 39 acres in 1838 when occupied by Joseph Martin. It was bounded at that time by Ynysderw, Tir y Bont and Ynysmeudwy Isaf. In 1861 the occupier was Jacob Lewis, owner of the Pontardawe chemical works. His grandsons, William and Lewis Harry Lewis, later lived in the property which was demolished around 1907 in order for the Public Hall and Institute to be constructed. Soar Calvinistic Methodist chapel (opened 1866), the gasworks (established 1869/70), Tawe Terrace (built 1911) and the Pontardawe sheetworks (built 1921) were also erected on Ynysygelynen land as was Orchard Street (pre-1877) and Fuller Street, both built on Cae Pandy.

Brynheulog estate, looking across from Cwm Du Glen, *c.* 1950. In the foreground lie some of the Maes Iago cottages. Alltycham House can be glimpsed (top centre) among the trees on the foothills of Craig Llangiwg (colloquially known as 'The Barley', itself derived from Birlip Hill).

Jacob Lewis (1803-70). Second son of Lewis and Mary, tenants of Pontardawe flour mill. Jacob was born in Llandeilo and was a draper by trade, owning a business in Castle Bailey Street, Swansea, in 1828 and (until 1831) a tea and grocery concern in the town. He lived at Castle Bailey Street in 1851 and established the Pontardawe chemical works during that year, on Pontardawe Mill Lands owned by Howel Gwyn. He subsequently moved to Pontardawe and made Ynysygelynen his residence. He married Elizabeth (née Pollard) on 24 June 1828 and they had ten children. Jacob was a local councillor for Upper Ward, Swansea from at least 1857. He also served as a poor law guardian, sat on the Swansea Infirmary Committee and acted as secretary to the committee of the Ancient Order of Druids.

Elizabeth Lewis (1806-83), wife of Jacob and born Elizabeth Pollard at Morriston, the youngest child of Joseph and Margaret. Joseph was brought up a Baptist but in 1801 joined the Society of Friends becoming a lively and instructive Quaker minister. An accountant by profession his other children were: Thomas, Mary, Margaret, Joseph, Benjamin, Anna and William. The latter was a noted painter of china, some of whose work is in the Victoria and Albert Museum and the National Museums & Galleries of Wales. Elizabeth continued to live at Ynysygelynen after her husband's death. She died on 14 April 1883 and, like Jacob, was buried at St John's church, Clydach.

Lewis Griffith Lewis (1830-1920), second son of Jacob and Elizabeth, pictured with his grandson Lewis da Costa Ricci. Lewis married Elizabeth Sarah Fear in June 1859 and soon after moved into Brynheulog, which he had built. By his will of 1907 he bequeathed ownership of the chemical works to his two sons. Lewis da Costa Ricci (1886-1967) was the son of Anselmo and Ida Gwendoline da Costa Ricci (see p. 56). He married, in June 1915, Harriet Marguerita Scott. He adopted the pen-name, 'Bartimeus', under which he wrote stirring tales of naval life and adventure. He changed his surname by deed poll in 1941 becoming Lewis Anselmo Ritchie. He was press secretary to George VI during 1944-47 and was knighted (KCVO) in 1947. He died on 7 February 1967, *The Times* obituary describing him as the 'kindest of men, rather shy and retiring of disposition'.

Elizabeth Sarah Lewis (1835-1903). Born Elizabeth Sarah Fear in Neath on 4 November 1835, eldest child of John Simmons Fear, a Neath ironmonger and Elizabeth Watson of Carmarthen. Her two sisters were Maria Anna (1837-1922) and Ellen Jane (1839-1926). Following the death of their father, their mother married Thomas Stephen Sutton of Wiltshire. He was an iron merchant who carried out iron smelting and refining in Neath. Like her husband Elizabeth was buried at St Peter's church.

Lewis Harry Lewis (1860-1943), eldest son of Lewis Griffith Lewis. He was born at Brynheulog, later living at Ynysygelynen and subsequently at Clasemont (Morriston) and Carey Hall (Bryncoch). With his brother Sydney he assumed ownership of the chemical works following their father's death. He married Victoria Ellen Worthington in 1889.

Victoria Ellen Lewis (1870-1944), wife of Lewis Harry Lewis. Together they had had four children: Dorothy Ellen, Lewis Reginald ('Rex') aka Reginald Worthington, Ida Worthington and Phyllis Worthington.

Ida Gwendoline Lewis (1862-1943). Born at Brynheulog, she was the second child of Lewis Griffith Lewis and sister of Lewis and Sydney. She married Anselmo da Costa Ricci in April 1885 and lived in London during her married life. After Anselmo's death she moved to a house named Glen-y-Mor in Pendine where she died. They had two children: Lewis da Costa Ricci (see p. 54) and Anna Russell da Costa Ricci (1887-1976). The latter married Geoffrey Charles Sankey.

Anselmo da Costa Ricci (1859-1916), husband of Ida Gwendoline Lewis. He was the Under Secretary to the Portuguese Financial Commission and son of Baron Anselmo Jose da Costa Ricci (1820-1903) who had been financial agent to the Portuguese government. Anselmo's mother was Anna Russell da Costa Ricci (née Barnes). Anselmo died in South Africa.

Sydney Sutton Lewis (1864-1958), c. 1950. The third child of Lewis Griffith and Elizabeth Sarah Lewis, he married Florence Margaret Thornley, his second cousin, on 28 December 1905. They lived initially at Trebanos House before residing at Brynheulog. They had two daughters: Florence Elizabeth and Lorna Gwendoline. With his brother, Harry, he owned the Pontardawe chemical works following the death of their father. A JP, he died on his ninety-fourth birthday and was buried at St Peter's church. He had taken a special interest in the work of the choir and Sunday school there and was keenly interested in the application of music in church services. There is a memorial for Sydney on the north wall of St Peter's.

Florence Margaret Lewis (1872-1961), wife of Sydney. She was the eldest child of Robert Thornley, a merchant in the Birmingham area and Anna Jennet, the latter being the third child of Griffith and Margaret Lewis of Alltycham (see p. 102). Among Florence's six brothers and sisters were: Lewis, who became a doctor; Vernon, who was a mining engineer and director of the South Wales Primrose Coal Company and Hedley's Collieries among others; Stanley, who rose to the rank of Commander in the Royal Navy and was awarded the DSO and Hubert, who became a Clerk of the Peace and Clerk to the North Riding of Yorkshire County Council for forty-three years and was knighted in 1958.

Florence Elizabeth Lewis (1906-94), gets into her 1931, 4-litre Bentley outside Brynheulog in August 1969. Alongside is her great-nephew Nicholas Ritchie. Elizabeth was the eldest daughter of Sydney and Florence Lewis. In her youth, Elizabeth enjoyed tennis, horse-riding and skiing. Her greatest passion though was cars, especially Bentleys. She regularly attended Bentley Drivers' Club events in her own 4-litre and was a marshal at the annual vintage Bentley races at Silverstone until well into her seventies. During the Second World War she took a first aid course and became a volunteer ambulance driver. President of the Pontardawe Nursing Cadets, she spent many years nursing first her mother and then her father. She left Brynheulog on 30 September 1973.

Lorna Gwendoline Lewis (1913-81), c. 1968. Youngest daughter of Sydney and Florence Lewis and born at Brynheulog where she lived until 1968, the year she married Howell Hamer. The great love of her life was horses and she subsequently lived at her Arab stud farm near Hereford where she died in 1981. Like her sister Elizabeth she had a great sense of fun, had a wide circle of friends and was well respected in Pontardawe. She served as a Wren during the Second World War.

Seven

Streets

Tawe Terrace and the Fairfield site, *c.* 1945. Tawe Terrace was built in 1911 on Ynysygelyen land. Although most of the houses have been pebble-dashed in recent years many will recall the distinctive circles that appeared on the property frontages which led to the terrace being known colloquially as 'Dartboard Street', 'Circle Street' and 'Target Row'. Note the corrugated sheeting (a product of the adjacent sheetworks) which demarcated the terrace from the Fairfield. Much of the latter's area was redeveloped in 1959 as the new bus depot of the South Wales Transport Co. Ltd. The trucks at the bottom are from the Hendy Merthyr Colliery in the Lower Clydach valley which closed in 1960.

Alltywerin Road, Pontardawe, *c.* 1925. These houses were constructed under the 1924 Housing Act and built on Alltycham farmland. 547 houses were erected by the Pontardawe Rural District Council at that time in Clydach, Craigcefnparc, Trebanos, Ynysymond, Ynysmeudwy, Ystalyfera, Alltycham, Alltwen, Rhos, Godre'r Graig, Cwmgors, Gwaun-Cae-Gurwen, Rhiwfawr, Cwmllynfell and Garnswllt, the majority being of the parlour type with three bedrooms. They were well designed properties and a great improvement on previous house types. Note the use of reinforced concrete for the boundary fences.

Gellygron Road, *c.* 1915. From at least the seventeenth century the land formed part of the Thomas of Gellygron estate. Early this century it was owned by Howel Gwyn Jeffries from whom it was acquired by Charles G. Gilbertson. The land was farmed by Gellygron 'home farm' which lay close to Gellygron House (whose boundary wall is to the right). This view shows the rural nature of the area at that time and contrasts sharply with the suburban development today. The field on the left now forms the private housing estate of Waun Fawr built by Barratt in 1995. Note also fields in the distance on which Waun Sterw, Alltywaun and Waun Penlan have been built. Before the first house on the right is the site of Rhyd-y-fro post office today and was formerly the Ryyd-y-fro branch of the Alltwen and Pontardawe Co-operative Society Ltd.

The Cross and High Street, Pontardawe.

Pontardawe Cross, c. 1960. A well known scene showing that traffic flow was still fairly moderate. The Cross Hotel, with its distinctive 'portico', closed around 1967. Next to the hotel on High Street was the 'Home & Colonial' (closed around 1970) – the Café on the Square today. 'Viv Date Carpets' (established 1984) occupies the site previously owned by Davies & Co., ironmongers.

Carpenters Row, Pontardawe, 1969. This was the first row of terrace houses to be erected in Pontardawe as the 'new' town was developing. They were built around 1830 and owned by Henry Leach of Plâs Cilybebyll primarily to house workers employed on the canal. The terrace consisted of six two-up and two-down properties – five houses and one public house. The Carpenters Arms ceased to function as a public house in 1925/26. The occupiers of the houses in 1946 were: Katie and David Jenkins (no. 2); Margaret and Glenys Harris (no. 3); Arthur, Rachel and Leslie Morgan (no. 4); Arthur and Maud Jones (no. 5) and George, Mary A. and Mary Holloway (no. 6). The properties became vacant in 1962 and were demolished around 1973.

Herbert Street, c. 1910, showing a traffic-free zone. The houses to the right, from the tall property towards us, were numbers 93-85 Herbert Street. These were demolished in the mid to late 1970s. Those beyond (numbers 95-101) were demolished around 1971 having been condemned as unfit for human habitation. The Jubilee Club now stands where the trees are, followed by numbers 100-130. Pontardawe railway station, Tanyrallt House and St John the Baptist's church, Alltwen, are conspicuous in the background.

Herbert Street, c. 1964. The 'Continental Café', 128 Herbert Street, was established in 1961 in what was, historically, Midland House and had been a drapery (Regent Buildings) owned by J.D. Owen between 1923 and 1955. The café proprietor was Antonio Cirillo who was held in great respect by the local community for his generosity and amiable disposition. It closed in 1968. Directly opposite the café was the Pontardawe Inn ('The Gwachel') which still survives and is pre-1869 in origin.

'The Avenue', Pontardawe, 1954. The Avenue Garage now stands on the right just before Adulum Baptist chapel. The Avenue formed part of Ynysderw House and was the scene of the 'monkey parade', with groups of girls and boys displaying their charms. The banner advertises that year's National Eisteddfod held in Ystradgynlais.

High Street, Pontardawe, c. 1908. The majority of the buildings shown are still in existence but have been put to alternative uses. The major change has been the replacement of the large stone wall on the left, which was the boundary of Gravel Bank House – the brewery manager's house and offices (demolished in the late 1960s). John Evans was living there in 1890. At the crossroads can be seen the original Cross Hotel, a two-storey building with a canopy at its entrance. The hotel was enlarged to its present dimensions in 1908. The effect of horse-drawn traffic is much in evidence!

Chemical Road seen from 'Station Hill', March 1970. The former LMS railway stores building lies to the left and beyond that is 'Min-yr-Afon', a private residence built virtually on the site of the Pontardawe flour mill. One of the lorries of Russell Davies, haulage contractor, can be seen in the far distance. As well as Russell Davies, Thomas Allen and James Hemphill had businesses on the former chemical works site.

Gwyn Street, Alltwen , c. 1910. The thoroughfare was formerly known as Queen Street but was changed in the 1870s in recognition of the pervasive influence of Howel Gwyn, the landowner, on the community. The 1891 census enumerator's return revealed 25 dwellings in Gwyn Street occupied by 116 persons. Thirteen heads of household were associated with coal mining while others included blacksmiths (2), labourers (2), an ostler, a rollerman and a signalman. The view remains much the same today but it is worth noting the single cold water tap, to the left, and the gas lighting – both features long gone.

These two views of Alltwen Hill were taken between 1900 and 1910. The earlier photograph (bottom) looks up the hill and shows the 'rural' character of the area. The start of Mill Row is to the right. The later photograph is a view down the hill showing (top right) the former post office. This closed in 1985 having been run for many years (until 1983) by Mrs Peggy Williams. Half-way down the hill, on the right, was the third site of the Alltwen branch of the Alltwen & Pontardawe Co-operative Society Ltd. It opened around 1910 as a drapery and boot stores, later selling food and general provisions. It closed in 1981/82 and is the Spar today, opened 1989. The Cross Hands public house (demolished 1975) is just visible at the bottom of the hill. Note the distinct lack of traffic in both photographs compared with today's congested thoroughfare. This remarkably straight part of Alltwen Hill is pre-1838 in origin and bisected Alltwen Common, which seems to have been enclosed in the 1830s.

Lloyd Street, Trebanos, looking towards the Daren colliery, *c.* 1962. A pre-1898 thoroughfare, it was built on Graig Trebanos land and may have taken its name from W. Lloyd who occupied Graig Trebanos in 1885 (later Trebanos House). There were four properties there in 1918: 'Isycoed', 'Wood Villa', 'Rosedene' and 'Myrtle Hill'. The property immediately left is 'Rockmead'.

Bethesda Row, Ynysmeudwy, *c.* 1930. These houses were also erected by the Pontardawe Rural District Council under the 1924 Housing Act. At that time the gardens extended down to the main road as is evident from the privet hedges at the front of the properties. The houses were of the garden village type, designed to a high standard with parlour, three bedrooms, kitchen, gardens to front and rear, porches at the entrances, and built with protruding L-shape façades to break up the monotony of flat-fronted terrace-style properties.

Eight
Houses, Buildings and Shops

Alltycham House. An 'ancient' site described in 1584/85 as 'Alltdracham', it was possibly the former home of the fourteenth-century bard and patriarch Hywel Melyn. The earliest recorded reference is 1513 when it was described as 'Allte acham' and was conveyed in that year by Grefithe ap John ap Grefith to Hopkyn ap Rees ap Thomas and Hopkyn ap Grefithe ap Ieuan ap Gwilym. It later became part of the Gellygron estate of the Thomas family but was bequeathed in 1733 by Mary Williams, the daughter of Richard Thomas of Gellygron and wife of Griffith Williams of Ynysderw, to her nephew Thomas Mathews of Nydfwch. It became part of the Penllergaer estate from 1750 but from around 1837 was owned by Josiah Rees, son of the famous Arminian minister of Gellionen chapel, and occupied by the former's brother, Richard Rees. From around 1853 it was in the possession of Griffith Lewis (see p. 102), coal proprietor and part owner with his brother-in-law John Morgan of Gellygron of the Primrose Colliery Company. Most of the property's features today date from Griffith's time who probably commissioned the noted local building contractor, John Griffiths of Alltwen, to undertake extensive modernisation. The property was subsequently owned by Griffith's daughter Mary Ann Lewis who married Ernest Hall Hedley, the latter living there until the First World War. Later occupants included Thomas Dixon (from whom the ascription 'Dixon's Farm' is derived), Archibald Harper (a renowned radiologist) and Dafydd Rowlands (former Archdruid of Wales).

Garth covered 142 acres in 1838 when owned by Evan Jones whose descendants remain there, the family being in ownership for some 350 years. In 1584/85 it was owned by Llewellyn John ap Hopkin ap Griffith. Garth is one of the key properties in Llangiwg parish, the estate also comprising Cwmllynfell Farm and Gellyluog Isaf, the latter in Llangyfelach parish and Rhyndwyglydach district. 100 acres of Garth land was sold to the National Coal Board in the early 1950s for the establishment of Abernant colliery, much of which has been re-acquired since the closure of the colliery in 1988.

Ynysmeudwy House, 1985. It was built by Michael Martyn Williams and William Williams in 1848. The mansion was constructed as the offices of the Ynysmeudwy Brickworks and Pottery Company but also served as the home of the Williams family. The house came into the ownership of the Ynysmeudwy Tinplate Company in 1882. Mr Frank Phillips, a director of the tinplate works then occupied the property. The premises were purchased by Mr and Mrs Richard Owen in 1967 and they opened it as the Glanafon Country Hotel in 1971. Many local groups used the 'Glanafon' as a meeting place: the Swansea Valley Rotary Club, Inner Wheel, Clwb Cinio. The Cwmtawe 7s was also launched from there. Shirley Bassey, Acker Bilk, Carwyn James and Max Boyce were among the celebrities who visited the establishment. Sadly the hotel burnt down in mysterious circumstances on 24 May 1991 and was subsequently demolished.

Glynteg, *c.* 1965. This was built in 1890 by Frank W. Gilbertson as his residence on the north side of the ravine of the Upper Clydach River, opposite Glanrhyd. Historically it lay on Llain Coed, part of the Gellygron estate. Frank's son-in-law and daughter, Mr and Mrs Hugh Vivian, were resident there in 1920. It was later tenanted by, among others, Captain and Mrs G.W.A. Doe (from approximately 1925 to 1950) and from, approximately, 1955 to 1974 by Mr and Mrs Danny Suff. It has been a private nursing home, 'Broadhaven', since 1986.

Danygraig House. Built in the 1870s on Ynysderw farmland this was the first home of Arthur and Ellen Gilbertson before their move to the purpose-built Glanrhyd between August 1877 and August 1878. In 1881 Danygraig was the abode of the solicitor David Bevan Turberville and his family. In 1891 Godfrey Wolf, clerk in holy orders, lived there. Various other tenants have occupied it since the First World War. In 1957 the property became the HQ of the Pontardawe District Girl Guides while in 1962 Pontardawe RFC were unsuccessful in establishing the site as a rugby clubhouse. It later served briefly as a Sunday school for All Saints church before conversion into flats in the late 1960s.

Gwrhyd Smallpox Hospital, c. 1932. The hospital (left) was established in 1928 to treat smallpox sufferers. It was a zinc structure and was only operational for a limited period being demolished at the time of the Second World War. Caretaker at one time was Daniel Griffiths of Railway Road, Cwmllynfell, his wage being 7s a week. The caretaker was expected to keep the wards well aired and ensure that fires were kept alight at least twice a week. He also had to arrange that his family be made 'secure from infection either by removal or otherwise'. He occupied the adjoining dwelling house (right) which was formerly Gwrhyd mixed infants school (closed 1906). The first mistress, Matilda Thomas, commenced duties on 13 January 1890. She found 'the children in a very backward condition [and] therefore decided to teach them the elementary subjects only, for a time'.

The Lyric cinema, c. 1960. The Lyric was originally a reading room, opened in 1869. It later became a Rechabite hall and a concert hall. Under the Cinematograph Act 1909 the building became a cinema, being licensed as 'The Palace' on 30 September 1914. The first licensee was J.J. Mathias of Aberavon. It had a seating capacity of 570, 3 exits and a wooden floor with lighting provided by a combination of electric and gas. F.T. Evans became licensee in 1930, the establishment becoming known as 'The Lyric' in 1931/32. It closed in late 1970, one of the last films to be shown being *Horrors of the Black Museum*. The final proprietor was Mr Bertie Bynorth. In 1995 the upper floor was converted to flats with a chemist's shop on the ground.

The Time Office, Ynisderw Road, 1939. The Time Office served the steel and tinplate works and was strategically located at the entrance to both. All 'time' workers had to enter the works' via the Time Office passageway that housed three clocks – the 'clocking-in' mechanism. Every 'time' worker had a card and works number. The office was thus an information centre important for the maintenance of attendance records, punctuality, hours worked and authorised overtime. There was a timekeeper for each shift, including Arthur Williams, Howel Daniels and David Williams or 'Dai Win the War'. The office was a centre for patrol work during the Second World War and in later years, night watchmen used the premises particularly when the works were idle. The office, having been derelict for several years, was demolished around 1972. The houses shown are nos 35 and 33 Ynisderw Road.

Eastmans Limited, *c.* 1905. This family butcher's shop was situated in the building that was recently occupied by the Canal Restaurant (destroyed by fire in 1997). Note the prime steak at 8d per pound! The lovely gas light would probably not escape the attention of vandals today. The building later became a drapers owned variously by Matt Harris and the Laviers. It was Ellis' the drapers from the late 1930s to the early 1970s, established by John Ellis.

Ale & Porter Stores, High Street, Pontardawe, c. 1900. Ann Davies was the licensee at that time and is probably the lady in the doorway. In the 1891 census enumerator's return the innkeeper, David Rees, was a widower. His nephew, Richard Davies, a rollerman, also lived there. The stores survived until the 1930s when it was replaced by the 'Home & Colonial'. The latter closed around 1970 and the 'Café on the Square' arrived.

Dillwyn Arms, Pontardawe, c. 1920. This was the third building of the name to occupy the site. The first was a thatched cottage, built around 1813. The second was a much larger building erected in the mid-Victorian period and spelt 'Dilwyn' in 1851. The third and present building is basically the Victorian structure with an Edwardian extension in red brick forming the new front. The group of workmen are probably Gilbertson's employees.

Davies & Co. Ironmongers, 1979. Situated at the Cross, this shop was a major landmark for 126 years. It was built in 1854 by William Evans for Messrs Davies & Co. as a general ironmongers and seed merchant. It closed in 1980, the premises becoming a carpet warehouse; initially 'Swansea Valley Carpets' and from 1984, 'Viv Date Carpets'. Both photographs were taken in 1979. Shown above, from left to right, are: Wynne and John Davies (the owners) along with employees Avis Williams and Griffith Evans (there for 40 years). Below is an excellent shot of Wynne and John as well as the shop's interior with its panoply of paint, electrical spares and tools. The shop also sold 'Corgi' toys.

Clatworthy's, watchmaker and jeweller, 33 Herbert Street, Pontardawe, c. 1967. The business was established by Thomas Clatworthy, a watch and clock maker from Pontypridd, prior to 1876. In 1881 Thomas, aged sixty, was living at the premises with his wife, Mary, aged sixty-two and their son, John, aged nineteen and also a watchmaker. Clatworthy also had premises at Ystalyfera and Swansea during the 1870s. Esme and Benjamin Clatworthy ran the Herbert Street business in 1974 but Benjamin died in that year. Esme managed the shop from 1975 to 1985 when she finally disposed of the premises, after which it became part of the 'Pink Geranium' wine bar establishment.

It was usual for jewellers to make their own time pieces during that period and not just sell ready-made clocks and watches. Ths silver fob watch was made by Thomas Clatworthy and assayed at Birmingham in 1876.

Steve Doyle's butcher's shop, High Street, Pontardawe. An attractive shop front with very distinctive decorative tiles depicting that the premises was a butcher's shop. The façade was typical of the 1920s with curved glass windows and green tiles. J. and G. Rees were the first butchers to occupy the shop from 1920 to 1940 with Steve Doyle, from Clydach, carrying on a butchery business from 1948 to 1991. The property is currently a barber's.

Parry's (below, right), 1974. Owned by Islwyn and Olive Parry from 1949 to 1974, it thrived as a newsagent, grocer and confectioner in the lower part of Herbert Street (no. 118). In its heyday it was strategically placed to capture customers from the steel, tinplate and sheet works as well as passing trade. Every manner of general provision was packed into the premises. In 1960 the adjoining property (no. 118b) was acquired for storage. The latter had also been a confectionery store run by Alice Powis and Edwin and Phyllis Harris. Both properties were demolished in 1975/76 as part of the new road construction in the area.

J. Bendle, boot and shoe maker, 103 Herbert Street, *c.* 1920. The building was situated off the main road and nestled between the latter and the Upper Clydach river. It was owned by Joseph Bendle who lived here with his wife Minnie and family. There were several such establishments in Pontardawe at that time, another six in Herbert Street alone: Cash & Co., W. & A. Clarke, Dan Davies, William Davies, David Lloyd & Sons and Thomas Martin Pugh. Two other businesses existed in High Street belonging to William Davies and Mrs David Rees. The Bendle establishment ceased trading in the late 1930s and appears to have been demolished during the Second World War.

The last surviving buildings in this part of Herbert Street, 1977. On the right is the former premises of Arthur Evans, ironmonger (115 Herbert Street) while, nearest, was the bakery concern of D.E. James ('James the Baker') at 117 Herbert Street. Both establishments were soon to be demolished like the private residences numbered 119 and 121 Herbert Street which had occupied the open space to the left. Large-scale demolition of the lower part of Herbert Street was necessitated by the construction of the new road bridge that year, part of which can be just seen to the right.

No. 10 Alltwen Hill was one of many small family-run shops in the village. It was owned originally by Mr Gwyn Jones (possibly the gentleman standing in the doorway) who opened it around 1910. Ownership then passed to Mr and Mrs Lewis Jones. In the 1940s the shop was rented by Gwyn Harris but his tenancy lasted only a short time, the premises subsequently closing. The property, along with various others such as the Cross Hands public house, were demolished in 1975 to make way for the new roundabout and realignment of Graig Road.

This shop was located in Gwyn Street, Alltwen and was formerly owned by Mr Joseph Roberts. It was run for many years by his daughter Eirlys Roberts and was known locally as the 'Shanty'. Pictured on the left is Mrs Mary Evans with Myra, her assistant, around 1930. Since 1985 the site has housed Alltwen post office run by Mr and Mrs Elfed Harris though they have been keeping a shop there since 1978. There was a property very close to this site in 1838 and it may be that, like that one, the shop's origin is associated with the Primrose Colliery Company whose tramroad ran just to the left of this picture.

Dressmaking and millinery shop, Trebanos, *c.* 1905. This was situated beneath what is now the Trebanos Working Men's Club and Institute, 99 Swansea Road. Dressmaking premises abounded in the days before mass production or when clothes could be bought 'off the peg'. In Pontardawe there were four such businesses at this time (not to mention several drapers and outfitters), all in Herbert Street: David Davies, J.C. Davies, Daniel Lloyd ('Manchester House') and William Thomas.

Lloyd's, confectioner and tobacconist, Trebanos, *c.* 1930. The shop was situated near the vestry of Gosen chapel. In later years one half was a fish and chip shop, the other sold sweets, newspapers and wool. It was called 'Siop Will Lloyd', William Lloyd being pictured here outside his shop. The business finally closed in the late 1970s and is now a private residence, 164 Clydach Road. At one time there were some eighteen shops in Trebanos.

Nine
Churches and Chapels

Saron Congregational chapel, Rhyd-y-fro. Erected on Rhyd-y-fro Mill land and opened in 1904, the land was donated by William Williams of Maesygwernen Hall, owner of the Upper Forest and Worcester tinplate works, Morriston and former MP. Two foundation stones were laid on 30 July 1904 by Miss Olwen Violet Williams of Maesygwernen Hall and Miss Mary Dulcibel Frances Gilbertson of Glynteg. This was the 'new' Saron, the original building, which still stands, having been erected in 1844. The contractor for the new chapel was J.R. Williams (Ystalyfera) whilst C.S. Thomas (Swansea) was the architect. The building cost £2,700. The first minister of the new chapel was the Revd J.R. Price. He was ordained at Rhyd-y-fro in July 1897 and his associates considered him a strong preacher, voracious reader and keen thinker who had a zeal for temperance. He died on 22 October 1934 aged sixty-six after giving thirty-seven years of faithful service. He was followed by Idwal Jones, R. Lloyd Davies, Caradog Williams, Harry Samuel and Walford Llewellyn, who has recently retired.

Adulum Baptist chapel, Pontardawe. Before Adulum was built the Baptists held services with the Wesleyans at Cae'r Doc school. The first chapel, built in 1845 on Ynysderw farmland, was a small, square, whitewashed building with a low pyramid roof and two rows of seats on the gallery. The first minister was the Revd Philip Morgan. The 1851 religious census revealed that the chapel had capacity for 96. The minister at that time was Charles Williams with Thomas John as deacon. The chapel was rebuilt in 1889, memorial stones being laid by J.T.D. Llewelyn of Penllergaer and Howel Watkins of Swansea, and by 1915 there were over 200 members. The chapel holds a weekly service but has been without a resident minister since J. Rowland Jones' time (1943-60).

Mount Elim Baptist chapel, Ynysmeudwy, c. 1980. A branch of Adulum opened in 1886, built on Ynysmeudwy Isaf land, the cause originally meeting at the Grosvenor, Herbert Street. The first minister or 'shepherd' was Mr Mathias, membership numbering 35. The second minister was Daniel Davies under whom membership increased by almost 100. Revd William Davies was pastor between 1924-47. The last Baptist minister was J. Rowland Jones. It has been an evangelical church since 1982, the first minister being David Sercombe. The present minister is Ian J. Parry.

New Church Temple, Ynysmeudwy. The New Church doctrines were based on the revelations of Emanuel Swedenborg (1668-1772), a Swedish scholar, scientist, practical administrator, legislator and man of affairs. The Society at Ynysmeudwy was the only one in Wales and owed its existence to seven founder members excluded from worship at Bethesda Independent chapel primarily for championing the cause of temperance. The church was built in 1890 on Ynysmeudwy Ganol land. The memorial stone was laid by John Bradford of Liverpool on 5 July 1890, the church becoming affiliated to the New Church Conference of Great Britain. The church closed in 1997 and has recently been sold.

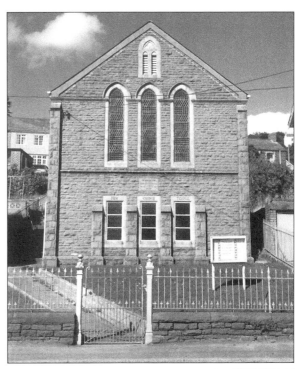

Bethesda Independent chapel, Ynysmeudwy, c. 1925. Built on Ynysmeudwy Uchaf land it opened in 1893, supplanting an earlier chapel nearby that had been built in 1861/62. A stone at the front of the chapel commemorates the tercentenary, in 1893, of John Penry, the famous Welsh Puritan. Revd J.T. Davies was the new chapel's first minister before leaving for Cymmer, Porth, in 1899. Services today are undertaken by Gareth Morgan Jones, of Tabernacle.

Ebenezer Independent chapel, Rhos, *c.* 1910. The cause started before 1896 as an offshoot of Alltwen Independent chapel, holding services in dwelling houses. A Sunday school opened in a little chapel, now the vestry, in February 1884, with an average attendance of eighty. With the opening of the New Primrose Colliery in 1895, Alltwen chapel allowed Rhos to go on its own. With membership increasing a new chapel, built on Cefn Celfi land, was completed and opened in 1905. Revd David Jenkins, Alltwen, was ordained as minister in 1897. He worked energetically during his fifty-year ministry, dying on 30 November 1947 aged eighty.

Bryn Seion Independent chapel, Gellinudd. It was built in 1896 and opened in June 1897, though long before this services had been held in the nearby Gellinudd Board School. After the death of Revd Rees Rees in 1910 the chapel was destitute of a pastor for five years until Revd W.J. Rees became minister of Alltwen. He served Bryn Seion well from 1915 to 1952 when he retired. During his ministry a small vestry for the children was built. John Henry Davies wrote, in 1967, 'After two world wars, brotherly love diminished and apathy prevailed. Many of the old members passed away'. The last chapel service was held in November 1993. The chapel was subsequently sold and the building is now a residential property.

Danygraig Independent chapel, 1909. A branch of Alltwen Independent chapel, Danygraig originated in 1886 in a Sunday school held in Alltwen Infants School which continued to be a spiritual home until the founding of the chapel in 1909. It was incorporated on 17 January that year by Revd Rees Rees and had 125 members. Members proceeded to erect a chapel to seat 600 and a vestry to accommodate 400 on land obtained from John Davies, ironmonger. The chapel, which cost £2,600, opened on 18 October 1910. Services are still held though there is no longer a resident minister, the most recent being E. Cadfan Philips (1983/84).

Danygraig chapel deacons, 1912. From left to right, standing: Thomas Jones, David R. Lewis, Evan Thomas (secretary), Thomas Lewis, William R. Morgan. Seated: John Thomas, James Hinkin, Revd Llewelyn Bowyer (minister), Thomas Richards, Owen Mathias.

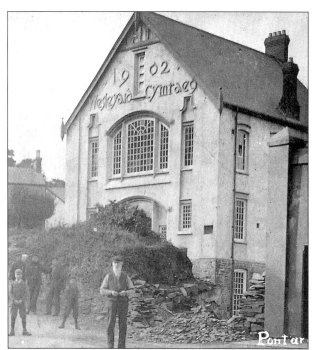

Horeb Welsh Wesleyan Methodist chapel, Pontardawe, c. 1905. The original Horeb was opened in 1845 alongside (what is now) Glanrhyd Road. Sixty years later it was superseded by the 'new' Horeb built on Maes Iago (James Street). Three old thatched cottages (Llydiarty Fagwr) were pulled down to make room for the foundations. The chapel opened in 1905 with a seating capacity of 500. Mr John Davies, ironmonger, the Cross, donated an organ worth hundreds of pounds as a gift to the church on its opening and he was one of its main pillars. The preacher at the opening was Dr Jones, of Bangor. The chapel closed in 1997 and is currently for sale. The last minister was Revd Pamela Cramme.

Interior of Tabernacle Independent chapel, Pontardawe. The foundation stone was laid by Lord Glantawe on 18 August 1880 and the chapel was officially opened on 21 August 1881 when Revd J.T. Davies of Gosen (Trebanos) and Bethesda (Ynysmeudwy) and Revd Rees Rees, Alltwen, preached. J.T. Davies guided the church from 1881 to 1899 and was followed as minister by H. Seiriol Williams (1899-1941), W.T. Owen (1942-48), T. Elfyn Jones (1949-1963), T. Burgess Jones (1964-76) and Gareth Morgan Jones from 1977 to the present day.

English Wesleyan Methodist chapel, Holly Street, Pontardawe. The cause started on 8 February 1903 in the Rechabites Hall (later the Lyric cinema). The church, which cost £600, opened in Holly Street on 28 October 1906, the sermon being given by Revd David Young, Folkestone. Closing in May 1992, the congregation of a dozen or so moved to Horeb Welsh Wesleyan Methodist chapel, James Street. Services for the English Methodists were held there on Sunday afternoons until 13 August 1995 when the denomination finally ended in Pontardawe. The last minister at Holly Street was Revd Douglas Williamson and the final English Wesleyan Methodist minister at Horeb was Revd Alf Austin.

Elders of Gosen Apostolic church, Holly Street, Pontardawe, 1934. From left to right, standing: David John Williams, Thomas Evans, Stanley James, Morlais James, Victor Steadman, Harry Tibbs, Jack Jones. Seated: Mrs Elizabeth Ann Evans, Jack Meredith, George Evans, William James (pastor), John Extance, Mrs Diana Meredith, Mrs Florence Williams. Gosen was built in 1921, using voluntary labour and 'second-hand bricks', although there had been an 'Apostolic' congregation at Pontardawe since at least 1911. William James (1880-1954), the first overseer and pastor, emigrated to New Zealand in the early 1950s. Along with the brothers Daniel Powell Williams and William Jones Williams of Penygroes he was one of the founding fathers of the Apostolic Church, itself an outgrowth of the 1904-05 Religious Revival.

Gosen Independent chapel, Trebanos. Built in 1865 on former Graig Trebanos farmland the chapel was incorporated in 1869. Two neighbouring ministers, Revd Phillip Griffiths, Alltwen and Revd Esau Owen, Hebron, Clydach, supervised Gosen until 1879. With membership increasing it became necessary to build a larger chapel (1891). The old chapel, situated below the Colliers Arms, was later demolished to make room for a new vestry (Gosen Fach) built in 1912, the community centre today.

Capel-y-Graig, Trebanos (Unitarian). This was an offshoot of Gellionen chapel, and was founded in 1893. During the ministry of J. Fisher Jones (1891/92) the congregation was encouraged to build a 'more convenient chapel' in Trebanos. It opened on 8 November 1894, the temporary building Bron y Wawr, on Graig Road, being converted into a vestry for Sunday school and cultural activities. In January 1904, the congregation built a large vestry by the side of the chapel. A new manse was built in 1932 and a spacious new hall opened on 27 June 1938. In 1974, because of subsidence, the rear of the chapel, including the vestry, was demolished.

Saint Michael & All Angels church, Trebanos, built in 1912 for 'the spiritual provision of the English speaking inhabitants' of the rapidly developing Trebanos and to provide a Sunday school for the community. The foundation stone was laid on 12 May 1912 by Mrs H.N. Miers, wife of Henry Nathaniel Miers of Ynyspenllwch who had given the land. The stone for the building was quarried from Ynystawe and built by the Clydach contractor, John Arnold. Like St Mary's, Clydach, (consecrated 1905) St Michael's is a daughter church of St John's, Clydach (consecrated 1847), and is served today by Revd Timothy Hewitt.

Saint Mary's church, Ynysmeudwy. As a result of population growth and industrialisation there was an increasing need for a church at Ynysmeudwy particularly as there was no church between St Peter's in Pontardawe and Holy Trinity, Ystalyfera. The building programme had been sponsored by Mrs Illtyd Thomas of Glanmor. Unfortunately she died before the work started but the movement for its erection was carried on by her daughter Mrs F.W. Gilbertson. The church cost £3,200 and was built of Pennant stone, quarried locally. The builders were Price Bros of Cardiff and the architect, J. Cook Rees of Neath. It opened in 1913.

All Saints church choir, 1943. From left to right, back row: John Isaac Edwards, Morgan Davies, Sam Pugh. Third row: Edgar Jenkins, Ivor Harris, William Preece, Roy Davies, Charles Chilcott, William John Morgan, Joe Powell. Second row: J. Morse (standing), C. Pugh, John Moses, E. Edwards (choirmaster), Revd Gwyn Hopkins (curate), Mrs E.T. Thomas (organist), B. Baston, Eurig Roberts. Front row: -?- (kneeling), Hugh Davies, Ray Davies, Justin Davies, Dudley Davies, Clive Davies, Owen Roberts, Alan Williams. The final service at All Saints was held on 2 November 1997 and the church has recently been sold.

Combined choirs of St John the Evangelist's, Cilybebyll and St John the Baptist's, Alltwen, c. 1969. From left to right, back row: Mrs Beryl Moses, Mrs Mary Davies, Lionel Edwards, Roger Morris, Neil Bendle, Geoffrey Moses, Revd Haydn Moses (rector), Neil Kingdon, Bill Morris, Tom Canning, -?-, Mr Griffiths. Fourth row: Joe Breen, Denise Evans, Diane Evans, Pauline Jones, Stephanie Henwood, Jennifer Harris, Beth Thomas, Lyn Rees, Anne Morris, Sam Thomas, Bernard Thomas. Third row: Geoffrey Chart, Griffith Wyn Thomas, Catherine Morris, Jane Preece, Linda Moses, Marie Bodycombe, Judith Rees, Alan Lewis Jones. -?-. Second row: Michael Davies (fifth from left). Front row: Stephen Bodycombe (fifth from left) and Ann Jones (seventh from left).

Ten
Schools

Alltwen Primary School, 1958/59. From left to right, back row: Nigel Preece, Gareth Evans, Keri Thomas, John Danton, Michael Griffiths, Huw Morris, Alan Hale, Phillip Evans, John Jones, Robert Tierney. Middle row: Mr William John Thomas, Richard Tierney, Jeffrey Getvoldsen, Ann Davies, Helen Palmer, Caroline Thomas, Kathleen Henwood, Peggy Griffiths, Sian Munro, Ann Griffiths, Ann Davies, Mr Tom Ellis Hopkin (headmaster). Front row: Susan Williams, Maureen Tierney, Betty Ann Bale, Yvonne Thomas, Pat Davies, Marie Williams, Joyce Davies, Gwyneth Davies, Audrey Williams.

Rhos School, 1908. Opened on 10 November 1908, the school lay historically on Pen-yr-Alltwen farmland, owned at that time by Ll.B. Williams, the 'squire' of Alltwen. The first headmaster was Henry Jones. His assistants in the mixed department were David Jones, Clifford Morgan and Gwenllian Williams. The assistants in the infants department were M.J. Williams, G. Bowen and M. Williams. The mixed department children (115) came from Alltwen Mixed School while 55 the infants were also transferred. In 1909 the school roll was 193, although some children had since transferred back to the Alltwen Mixed School. All the boys in Standards 1-4 were taught mining.

Rhos schoolchildren, Standards 3 and 4, 1908. Note the hobnail boots!

Construction of Trebanos Infants School, 1909. It was built on Graig Trebanos land and opened the following year. In 1915 a junior department was erected, the two amalgamating as Trebanos Primary School on 1 September 1964. The school closed in July 1993 on account of subsidence fears but following a vigorous campaign mounted by local residents it re-opened in September 1997 to continue a fine educational tradition in the community.

Trebanos Junior School children in St David's Day outfits, 1952. From left to right, standing: John ?, Keith Price, Gwyn Williams, Alan Rogers, Brian Whettleton, Alan Matthews. Seated: Meriel Jones, Ann Walker, Maureen Bowen, Eryl Rees, Tegwen Williams, Janice Jones.

Tanyrallt School Football Club, 1895. The Pontardawe Collegiate School, Tanyrallt House, Alltwen, was established in 1868 and closed in 1896. Standing, left, is Astley W. Samuel, who, like his father William before him, was the school's principal. When it closed Astley became a Swansea auctioneer. Will Hopkin, later to become the founder of the *West Wales Observer*, is standing third from the left. Tanyrallt House was built around 1862 when it was the residence of Lewis Morgan (1839-65), eldest son of John Morgan (1802-68) of Gellygron, colliery proprietor.

Alltwen Infants School, class 2b, 1925. The school was built on two levels on Dyffryn Road in 1883. The most conspicuous feature are the arches built on the lower level tier which allowed the children to play under cover during inclement weather. The school closed in 1982 and was amalgamated with Alltwen Primary. The building is now the Alltwen Community Centre, owned by the Cilybebyll Community Council, who also use it as a venue for council meetings.

Rhyd-y-fro Board School was built by Henry Thomas in 1876 under the control of the Llangiwg School Board. It was erected on Rhyd-y-fro Mill land, obtained from A.V. Davies-Berrington for a rent of £2 per annum, and opened on 25 June 1877. Since that date the school has had only five headmasters, the first being Alfred Williams Owen. In 1904 the school became the responsibility of the Glamorgan County Council and David Morgan was appointed as acting headmaster. Mr D.J. Terry was appointed in 1922, followed by Miss Catherine Lloyd in 1951, Ken Lauder in 1964 and Wyn Griffiths in 1993. The original school closed in 1984 after new premises had been built at Waun Penlan.

Llangiwg Board School, girls' department, c. 1905. A violin class is pictured. The class was introduced in 1904 by Mr Whitaker from Swansea who taught 77 children. Annie Rees (née Chilcott) is second from the right in the second row. The school was opened in Brecon Road in October 1885. So many pupils attended that the establishment was divided into girls' and boys' departments; 400 pupils attended in 1887. In April 1899 Pontardawe Infants School was completed thus relieving some of the pressure on numbers. Miss Hannah A. Davies was headmistress of the girls' department for the whole of its existence until 1914 when it became the Pontardawe Girls School. She continued as headmistress until 1923.

Children of Pontardawe Boys' School, 1923. Note the variety of neckties. The Boys' School was opened in Smithfield Road on 2 March 1914, the original 'Boys' Department' having been part of Llangiwg Board School. The headmaster of the Boys' School in 1923 was T.R. Williams.

Pontardawe Secondary School, 1938. It opened in Smithfield Road on 6 September 1913 as the Pontardawe Higher Elementary School becoming in 1921 a county secondary school. The headmaster from its origin until 1946 was J.W. Thomas. It became Cwmtawe Comprehensive School in 1969. The following have been identified: from left to right, back row: Norman Extance (first), Howard Griffiths (sixth). Middle row: Barbara Ellis (first), Molly Milton (second), George Parker (fifth), Huw John (sixth), Gordon Williams (seventh). Front row: Renee Griffiths (first), Gwen Owen (fourth), Miss James (French mistress, centre).

Eleven
Personalities

David 'Papa' Thomas (1794-1882). Ironmaster of Catasauqua, Pennsylvania, USA, David Thomas was born at Ty Llwyd farm in the hamlet of Wern-ddu between Alltwen and Bryncoch. He married Elizabeth Hopkins of Cilhendre Fawr Farm, Alltwen with whom he had Jane, Gwenllian, Samuel and David. It was at Ynyscedwyn Ironworks in the Swansea Valley, where he was employed from 1817, that David Thomas became the first person in the world to successfully produce iron using anthracite coal as a fuel in combination with the 'hot blast' method of production. This consisted of forcing hot air into the furnace instead of the more usual cold air. He emigrated to America in 1839 and built the first successful American anthracite-fuelled blast furnace at Pottsville, Pennsylvania. He subsequently founded the Thomas Iron Company which became the largest producer of anthracite iron in America. Half of all the iron manufactured in the USA in the mid-nineteenth century was the result of David Thomas' invention. The New York Literary Album of 1869 made this comment of him: 'Probably no man has done more for the permanent prosperity of the United States than Mr Thomas, and his efforts of enterprise entitle him to a distinguished place amongst America's useful citizens'.

John Henry Davies (1887-1974), *c.* 1920, mining engineer, lecturer and historian. He attended the University College of South Wales and Monmouthshire between 1909-11 and gained a diploma in mining. In 1933 he became Principal of the Mining and Technical Institute and first headmaster of the Secondary Technical School for Boys, Pontardawe. A Fellow of the Geological Society, he was awarded the R.H. Worth prize in 1963 in recognition of his contributions and work on the stratigraphy of coal measures. A keen student of local history he wrote extensively on his adopted area, his *History of Pontardawe and District*, published in 1967, proving indispensable for those interested in the area's heritage. Leonara, who he married in 1919, was highly respected; she was a prominent figure in the public life of Pontardawe and was awarded an MBE in 1934 for her services.

'Bertie Milk' and 'Annie'. Bertie Williams delivered milk to Rhos, Gellinudd, Alltwen and Pontardawe from 1946 to 1973, taking over from his father William Williams, 'Will the Milk'. The family farmed the Banwen smallholding in Alltwen and later moved to Lletty Philip Farm, overlooking Rhos. Up to 1962, Bertie used a horse and cart and then a tractor and trailer to 1965, after which a Landrover became the principal means of transport. His three horses were called 'Sunny Boy', 'Tulip' and 'Annie Laurie'. More than once Tulip bolted while on the round. One incident was reported in *The South Wales Voice* on 1 March 1952 under the headline: 'Runaway Horse Stopped'. It is said that on another occasion a constable captured Tulip by commandeering a bread van and cornering the horse.

Inspector John Gibbon and family, Pontardawe, c. 1905. Inspector Gibbon was the sixth policeman to hold the rank of inspector at Pontardawe. He resided with his family at the police house attached to the police station on High Street and died while on the beat at Rhyd-y-fro in 1906. Pictured are Inspector Gibbon, his wife Harriet holding their child Polly, with their other two daughters Lizzie and Annie standing in front of them. Harriet's sister is on the right. John Gibbon is the grandfather of Hubert and Haydn Gibbon of Tawe Terrace, Pontardawe.

Mr and Mrs Henry John celebrate their golden wedding at the Victoria Inn, Pontardawe, 13 October 1927. They were married at St Peter's church in 1877 by its first vicar, David Jones. Over fifty of their friends, descendants and relatives gathered to enjoy the 'sumptuous repast' which had been prepared by their five daughters, the eldest of whom, Mrs Dan Davies with her husband, were then host and hostess of the inn. Henry was born in 1851 at Ynysmeudwy Isaf Farm. His grandfather was John Jones of Ynysderw Farm – 'Sion Ynysderw'. Henry's wife, Hannah, was the daughter of the publican and 'oracle', John Morgan of Alltwen, whose bardic name was 'Bardd Tawe'.

Captain Daniel Nicholas, *c.* 1890. Dan Nicholas was a Master Mariner in the merchant navy who later became a farmer at Ynysmeudwy Ganol Farm. He was born at Tresaer farm, Mathry, Pembrokeshire. A number of ships are recorded with Dan Nicholas as captain: *Elmira* in 1876, *Charlotte*, and *Andorinha*, which he is reputed to have owned. Dan was quite a character in the area. Whenever he was home from the sea he always flew a flag from the home he occupied, either Ynysmeudwy Ganol or later Tresaer House, Ynysmeudwy, which he built in 1890. When Dan died in 1902 his body was taken by horse and wagon from Ynysmeudwy to Mathry church for burial.

The *Andorinha, c.* 1880. This was a four-masted barque engaged in the coaling trade between Swansea and Australia. She is not flying a house flag denoting that the ship was owned by a shipping company, so she could have been owned by Captain Nicholas himself. The space below the main deck was for carrying coal or other bulky cargo. The accommodation was in the small cabins on the main deck or in the forecastle, the cabin in the bows. Behind the foremast was the galley where all meals were prepared. Officers lived in the stern quarters with the enclosed wheelhouse above. In 1906 the *Andorinha* was owned by Goldberg and Sons of Swansea. The painting was executed at New South Wales, Australia.

Pont Nicholas, Ynysmeudwy. Captain Nicholas resided at Ynysmeudwy Ganol for a time and the bridge crossing the canal giving access to the farm became known to the local inhabitants as 'Pont Nicholas'. The official name of the canal bridge is Ynysmeudwy Ganol Bridge and it was built in 1795/96. The majority of bridges and locks on the Swansea Canal were given local nick-names which reflected their ownership or use. Other examples are 'Works Bridge' (Pontardawe), 'Bryn Bridge' (Ynysmeudwy) and 'Pelican Lock' (Ystradgynlais).

D.R. Williams, MBE, (1896-1961). 'D.R.' was the son of J.R. Rees who ran Williams Bros (see p. 43). He became a partner in the 1930s and greatly expanded the business, particularly when he went to London shortly before 1939. There, he obtained government approval to become a nominated contractor allowing the firm to help build aerodromes. He became an Apprentice Master under the Swansea Valley Joint Apprenticeship Committee in 1946, building the first house in Pontardawe under this training scheme. It was said that nothing happened in Pontardawe without 'D.R.' being involved. He was president of the National and Wales Federation of Building Trade Employers and is shown wearing the chain of office of the Welsh Federation of Civil Engineering Contractors. His wife, Ethel (née James), was a former schoolteacher.

Canon T.R. Walters James (1905-77). A native of Ystradgynlais he gained a BA at St David's College, Lampeter in 1927 and was ordained in 1928. He was then curate of Llansamlet, Cockett and Glais before becoming vicar of Llanstephan and Boughrood from 1935-42 and St Luke's, Cwmbwrla, from 1942-51. He was latterly vicar of Llangiwg from June 1951 until his retirement in September 1975 being appointed Rural Dean for the Deanery of East Gower in 1958 and Canon of Brecon Cathedral in 1961. He was held in very high regard by the community while his ecumenical spirit endeared him to those of other denominations. His wife was Trixie and they had three children: Margaret, Tony and Noel.

William Griffiths, 'Ivander', (1830-1910). Choral conductor, adjudicator and temperance champion. The temperance movement stimulated choral singing in the Swansea Valley under the guidance of Ivander who moved to Pontardawe from his native Aberavon in 1850 to become a cashier in William Parsons' iron and tinplate works. He soon became responsible for local singing classes, attaching himself to the small Methodist cause in Trebanos – Tabernacle chapel – where he became secretary to the Sunday school. In 1853 he founded one of the earliest Bands of Hope in Wales and in 1854 established a temperance choir at Pontardawe. By 1862 this had developed into the Swansea Vallet Choral Union ((Aelodau Undeb Corawl Dyffryn Tawe) which became celebrated throughout south Wales because of its choral and congregational singing.

Aelodau Undeb Corawl Dyffryn Tawe, 1862. A grand reunion meeting of the choir was held on 5 July 1902 to commemorate the choir's fortieth anniversary. From left to right, back row: J. Alexander, W. Hinkin, D. Williams, A. Cornelius, M. Lewis, J. Davies, D.J. Jones, R. Jones, J. Morgan, L.H. Thomas, R. Pipe, J.W. Thomas. Middle: J. Thomas, J. Williams, D. Williams, T. James, R. Rees, Mrs A. Lewis, Mrs R. Williams, Mrs R. Rees, Mrs A. Emmanuel, Mrs H. Morgan, Mrs W. Evans, Mrs S. Stephens, Mrs H. Jenkins, Mrs M. Lewis, Mrs R. Rees, Mrs J.R. Jones. Front: W. Williams, J. Morgan, L. Williams, W. Phillips, W. Williams, M.H. Thomas, D.T. Prosser, W. Ivander Griffiths, Mrs W. Ivander Griffiths, W. Thomas, Revd W. Samlet Williams, W. Gwynne Smith, P. Jones, E. Jones, W. Evans.

Griffith Lewis (1814-87), sixth son of Lewis and Mary and younger brother of Jacob. He married Margaret Lewis at Ystradgynlais on 9 June 1837 and moved to Alltycham around 1853. He was a coal proprietor who, with his brother-in-law, John Morgan of Gellygron, owned several mining concerns in the locality, notably Waunycoed, Cwmnantllwyd and the New Primrose. They also owned the Ynysmeudwy Pottery for a time (1861-71). Mary Ann, his eldest daughter, married (in February 1881) Ernest Hall Hedley, JP, county councillor, mining engineer and colliery owner, the latter taking over his father-in-law's mining concerns on his death.

Harold Penderel (1896-1967), Garth, Rhyd-y-fro, 1950. One of the best known inhabitants of the Pontardawe district, Elton Augustus Harold Penderel was one of four sons of Mr and Mrs Thomas Jones of Garth, the family changing its name to Penderel by deed poll in the early 1930s. He served in both world wars and was one of the first to be enlisted to the Royal Tank Corps, where he fought at Cambrai and the Somme. Harold 'The Garth' became a well known, if not slightly eccentric figure, in the Swansea valley between the wars. He played in the pack for Swansea RFC in the famous 'All-Whites' team of the 1920s along with such personalities as Gwilym Michael and Rowe Harding. He also captained Pontardawe RFC. A keen local historian, he had a deep and abiding love for the parish church of Llangiwg which he served as vicar's warden for forty years.

Marie Hopkin (née Mainwaring). Marie, born in 1850, was the first registered midwife in Alltwen, receiving her certificate of registration from the Central Midwives Board on 26 May 1904. She had however been practising since 1901. Her record shows that she was in attendance for 486 births between 1911 and 1919. She married Dafydd Isaac Hopkin, a deacon of Alltwen Independent chapel and had three daughters: Elizabeth, Miriam and Margaret. She lived at 15 Dyffryn Road, Alltwen.

Martin John (1904-92), with his wife Mabel, in 1976. Born in Pontardawe, Martin John founded the Pontardawe Old Age Pensioners Association in February 1946. He also founded the Pontardawe Old Music Lovers Male Voice Party and was a founder member of the Swansea Valley OAP Area Council which included seventeen associations, half of which he had established. He subsequently became president of the National OAP Association of Wales. From 1955 he was responsible for organising annual eisteddfodau and singing festivals for senior citizens in the Swansea valley and many of his Welsh and English hymns have been included in the 'Gymanfa' programmes. He was awarded the MBE in 1979 for services to the elderly.

Gynla Panacz, a Hungarian exile who settled in Pontardawe after fleeing from his native country following the Soviet Union invasion in October 1956. Gynla was a sugar-beet factory worker in Hungary when the rising began in Budapest on 23 October. Along with his two brothers, Anthony and Geza, he rushed to arms. After the Soviet troops re-entered the country on 4 November they fought on until all hope was lost. Escaping, the brothers separated and went by different routes to various parts of the frontier, sleeping in snow and finding food wherever they could. Reaching Austria, Gynla was flown to London where he revealed he had another brother, Joseph, living in Pontardawe. He was promptly sent to the town. Within two days of arriving Gynla found a job with Richard Thomas and Baldwins Ltd as a mason's labourer.

Eva Harris (née Cook) started singing and reciting at eisteddfodau at the age of six. She has won first prize for *Penillion* singing at three national eisteddfodau – Neath (1918), Swansea (1926) and Treorchy (1928). Eva also won the Chair three years running at the Brechfa local eisteddfod for her poetry. While living in Coventry she formed a ladies choir, The Gwalia Singers, which comprised fellow Welsh exiles. Her devotion to Welsh culture was rewarded when she was made a member of the Gorsedd at the 1992 national eisteddfod held in Aberystwyth. At ninety-two years of age, Eva looks forward to her continuing involvement with Welsh cultural life.

Twelve

Leisure and
Social Events

The Workhouse (now the Dan y Bryn Residential Care Home), 11 April 1907, on the occasion of the last meeting at the Institution of the Pontardawe Rural District Council and Pontardawe Board of Guardians. From left to right, back row: A.E. Edmunds (sanitary inspector), David Jenkins (relieving officer), R. Short (workhouse master), Daniel Thomas, Griffith Jeffrey. Fourth row: Will Hopkin (reporter), Samuel Morgan (Cwmtwrch), Rhys Williams, L.W. Francis, W.E. Parry, John Jordon (Glais). Third row: David James (Alltwen), Charles Bevan Jenkins (clerk), Dr John Jones, David Williams (Ystradgynlais), John Morgan (engineer), W.J. Jones (reporter). Second row: D.W. Davies, J.G. Harries, Wyndham Lewis (deputy clerk), Henry Thomas (Trebanos), D.M. Davies, Hopkin J. Powell, Thomas Rees (registrar), John Griffiths (Godre'r Graig). Front: John Powell (Abercrave), Tom Morgan (Ystalyfera), William Jenkins (Mawr), David Jones (chairman, Mawr), Dr George Jenkins (Clydach), Revd John Rees (Cwmllynfell), William Morgan (Ystradgynlais). The absentees were Herbert Lloyd, W.J. Percy Player, Johnny James, W. Hargreaves, Morgan Price and Tom Williams.

Pontardawe Rural District Council officers, 1957. From left to right, standing at back: W.R. Davies, Douglas Evans. Back row: -?-, Emi Francis, Betty Roderick Davies, Cyril Edwards, Sarah Lloyd, Elwyn Lewis, Lewis Williams, Eddie Hanford, Mr Mark, Irvin Rees, Arwyn Davies, Eurof Williams, -?-. Middle: Ieuan Lewis, Alwyn Rees, John Rogers, Howel Hopkin, Doug David, E. Lewis, Cliff Williams, Cliff Palmer, Shirley Edwards, Danny Davies, Miss Davies, Ann Booth Evans, Gaynor Walters. Front: Edwin Davies, E.D. Jones, P. Whittles, T.H. Wilson, D.J. Thomas, D.G. Meredith (clerk), D.S.F. Williams, May Jenner, Non Williams, Dorothy Harding.

Pontardawe Lodge of the Loyal Order of the Moose, c. 1952. The Pontardawe Lodge (no. 48) began in 1928 only three years after the first British lodge was formed in Tredegar. From left to right, back row: Len Pratley, David Randell Thomas (see p. 115), Tom Pratley, Lionel Cooke, Gordon Thomas. Middle: Bryn Lewis, -?-, Ben Williams, Evan John Davies, Tom Jones, Tom Jones' son, -?-, John Aaron Thomas, Eddie Hanford. Front: Jim Steadman, H. Joe Powell, David Williams (governor), Harry Pratley, Arthur Evans, Edwin Lewis (possibly holding granddaughter, Marilyn).

Employees from the Joint Works Committee of Richard Thomas and Baldwins Ltd, Pontardawe, present Gellinudd Hospital with a television set, *c.* 1958. Left to right: Gwen Pugh, Rhys Williams, Richard Cooper, Evan Davies, Maldwyn Davies, Alfie Evans, M. Rhys-Williams (matron), Archie Mumford, -?- (patient), Hilary Davies, Dan Young, D.W.H. (Howel) Childs. It opened in 1902 as an isolation hospital and was built on Gelligeiros land, part of the Cilybebyll estate. Today it serves as a rehabilitation centre for the elderly and also cares for the terminally ill.

Outside the old fire station, located to the rear of the former Pontardawe Rural District Council offices in Holly Street and showing an old 'Dennis' fire tender. The fireman is Jim Lewis of Alltwen, the boys are Huw Thomas (left) and Paul Morgan. The fire station closed in 1966/67, a modern station having been built on Alltycham Drive to provide necessary cover for Pontardawe and the surrounding districts. The old station premises were subsequently used as office accommodation by the Lliw Valley Borough Council.

Trebanos Silver Band, Caernarfon camp, 1912. Formed around 1890 it was one of several in the district. The brass band movement began in the north of England but spread to all parts of Britain where in Wales they were prominent in valley mining communities. Other notable bands in the locality were Alltwen, Pontardawe, Gwaun-Cae-Gurwen and Ystalyfera. The instruments shown were typical of such ensembles: cornets, euphoniums, tenor horns, trombones, basses, side and base drums. There was no difference between a 'brass' band and a 'silver' band except for the colour of the plating on the instruments.

Alltwen Silver Band, c. 1903. This band were champions Second Class of the South Wales Association and won numerous prizes. From left to right, back row: Tom Morgan, Lewis John Lewis, Llewelyn Lewis, Astley W. Samuel, Phil Palmer, Arthur Davies, Harry Mumford. Middle: Alfie Powell, Harry Thomas, John Gibbs, Morgan Davies, Evan John Davies, John Rees, John Price, Thomas John Davies, Will Davies. Front: Wat Rees, John James, Willie Davies, Richard Davies, Tal Davies, Russell Davies (conductor), Tom Morgan, Trevor Thomas, Idris Davies, Willie Griffiths. On floor: Tom Sterl and Ernest Sterl.

Ynysmeudwy Miners Welfare Carnival, 21 July 1934. Annual carnivals were regular social events in the community. These were held on Ynysmeudwy Uchaf Farm fields and primarily comprised brass, silver and jazz band competitions in addition to fancy dress and beauty competitions. The winner of the beauty competition would have been designated the Carnival Queen and she would have been taken back to Pontardawe by canal barge. The carnival extended over four days and included a grand dance on the Thursday.

Pontardawe Carnival, 2 September 1933, with a male jazz band at the recreation field near the Glanrhyd tinplate works. The bands made their own costumes and practised regularly to achieve the desired standard of competence for the competitions. Many of the bands were very talented and it was considered a great honour to win at the carnival. The jazz bands originated in the United States and became commonplace in Britain during the 1930s. Most bands played the kazoo, sometimes referred to as a 'gazoota'. First prize in the jazz band competition was the sum of £15.

Pontardawe British Legion Women's Section, 1930. Women's sections have been a hallmark of the Royal British Legion since its inception in 1921. Included here are: Mrs Johnny Davies, Mrs Collins, Mrs Paynter, Mrs Powell, Mrs Andrews, Mrs A. Lewis, Mrs J.R. Williams, Mrs Banks, Mrs Knight, Mrs Pugh, Mrs Tucker, Mrs Grubb, Mrs Bradley, Mrs Smith, Mrs Harding, Mrs Danton, Mrs Weaver, Mrs B. Jones, Mrs Jones (Rhos), Mrs Bayford, Mrs Gladys George, Mrs Curran, Mrs W. Jones, Mrs M. Thomas, Mrs Hancocks, Mrs Laura Jones, Mrs S. Rees. Peggy Collins is the child in the front row.

Pontardawe Ladies Choir about to board a bus in Dynevor Terrace for Talgarth to give their annual concert at (and in aid of) Talgarth Sanatorium, 1946. Generally, from left to right: Blodwen Morgan, Bess Lewis, Catherine Rees, Maggie Rees, Mary Phillips Jones, Rebecca Davies, Megan Rees Thomas, Gwyneth Rees, Nancy Jones, Mrs Cyril Griffiths, Mary Rees, Gwennie Evans, Mrs John Emlyn James, Jennet Jones, Lena Rowlands, Hillary Lewis, Mrs Sydney Davies, Carrie Williams, William Rees (conductor), Mary Davies, Dilys Davies, Nina Davies, Elisabeth Ann Evans, Mary John, Mary Williams, Mrs W.R. Davies, Mrs Tom Thomas, Hetty Jones, Clara Chilcott (reporter), Katie Lewis, Mrs Rogers, George David and Hopkin John.

Pontardawe Male Choir, Paddington Station, February 1939. Among those pictured are: William Williams, Elfet Jones, Hopkin John, Glyn Price, Sylvanus James, Arthur Gwyn Davies, Tom Harries, Evan John Davies, Richard Cooper, William Henry Davies, Idris Jones, Jack Williams, Islwyn James, David Daniel (conductor), Luther Lewis, Wynn Jones, Glyn Lewis, -?- , -?-, Glyn Davies, -?-, Willie Rees, Rees Morgan, Oswald Davies.

Coronation party, West Crossways, Pontardawe, 1953. Among the party-goers pictured are: Bessie Ward, Mr and Mrs Tony Aleman, Mr and Mrs Dai Knight, Mr and Mrs Tom Bodycombe, Mrs Landry, Mrs Beddoe, Mrs Beryl Morgan, Mrs Trollope, Mr and Mrs Ford, Mrs Matthews, Myra Jones, Mrs Williams and Ann, Mr and Mrs Alcwyn Rees, Mr and Mrs Viv Lewis, Des and Doreen, Mrs Ayres, Bill and Betty Davies, Mr and Mrs Jeffries, Jim and Dora Rees, Betty and Mrs Thomas.

Pontardawe nursing cadets, St John's Ambulance Hall, *c.* 1960. Pictured, among others, at the back (with hat) is Miss Elizabeth Lewis of Brynheulog, President of the Pontardawe Nursing Cadets and second from right, back, Miss Hannah Gittus, one of the service's stalwarts. The ambulance hall was built in the early 1930s. The hall not only served the Order of St John but provided facilities for many other organisations. The Pontardawe branch of the St John Ambulance Brigade was formed in 1912 and started as a first aid class under Dr W. Owen Evans.

Alltwen operetta, *Dick Whittington and his Cat*, the Gwyn Hall, April 1960. The operetta was performed by members of St John the Baptist's church, Alltwen, having been written and produced by Revd Rees Emmanuel, rector of Cilybebyll, at back, right. Six performances were given, none of the participants being over fourteen. Margaret Jones played the 'Lady Mayoress', Peggy Griffiths was the 'Fairy Queen', Beti Wyn Richardson was 'Dick', Gregory Evans was the 'Cat', James Jones was the 'Executioner', Ian Preece was the 'Lord Mayor', Freddie Bartlett was 'Matilda, the Stowaway', and Malcolm Henwood was the 'Demon King'.

'The Gwachel' racing stable, c. 1920. Alan Phillips, long standing proprietor of the Pontardawe Inn or 'Gwachel', had, together with his wife Mary (affectionately known as 'Aunty') a stable behind the pub. He had a succession of trotting ponies, one of which was 'Butcher's Lad' who became Welsh champion. George Phillips, Alan's uncle, who was decorated for bravery in the First World War is seen here. Alan Phillips came to be held in 'great popularity for his geniality and interest in sport'. He died in the 1970s.

Motorcycle club at All Saints Cottage, Glanrhyd Road, c. 1930. Five sets of sidecar combinations and two single bikes. Four of the sidecars are identical but the car on the right has a wicker body. Manual horns and carbide lamps were standard on all machines. The registration of the right hand machine is CH63.

Alltwen recreation ground was founded in 1922. It was located to the south of the junction of Park Road and Lon-y-Wern. Access was obtained via a steep narrow path which crossed the Nant Llechau. The park comprised a tennis court, children's play area, bowling green and pavilion. The bowling green is seen here in its heyday in the early 1950s with the bowls pavilion in the background. Left is Sammy Thomas, posing with Mr Gibbs, both of Alltwen. The recreation ground was derelict by the early 1960s, however, and a valuable asset was thereby lost. The original Alltwen Recreation Ground Committee comprised nine trustees. Its last meeting took place at Alltwen chapel vestry on 16 April 1962.

Pontardawe mixed tennis team, c. 1904. The team played at the beginning of the century, probably at Glanrhyd which appears to be the property seen here. It was the home of Arthur Gilbertson whose family were great local patrons of the game. On the back row, third from left, is Charles Giddings next to Ivor Harris (fourth). Sixth from left is Albert Davies (of 'Davies the Ironmongers', The Cross) next to Phillip Lewis (a grocer, seventh) and John Parker Lewis (eighth). On the front row, second from the left is Maggie Jane Harries.

'Mr Gilbertson's Cricket XI', 1903. From left to right, standing: Harry Thomas, T. Lewis, D. Evans, T. Jones, B. Thomas, W. Jeremiah, J. Jenkins, D. Lewis (secretary). Seated: A. Bodycombe, A. Davies (vice-captain), Charles G. Gilbertson, Arthur Gilbertson (president), John Herbert Purdon Lloyd (captain). The latter was of Plâs Cilybebyll and was the eldest son of Herbert Lloyd. On 10 April 1964 the *West Wales Observer*, in reporting the funeral of Harry Thomas, stated that he was '...the only surviving member of Mr Gilbertson's XI cricket team. He was proud of a photograph of the team which was taken outside Glanrhyd House'.

Ben Thomas (1891-1961) with his son David (1920-94), in 1922. Ben holds the bat with which he scored 1,000 runs for Pontardawe Cricket Club in the 1921 West Wales League season. Ben captained the team and eventually became chairman of the club. After his cricketing career he entered local politics and was elected to the Pontardawe Rural District Council. He was chairman of the council in 1946.

Gilbertsons' Welfare AFC, Welsh League, 1936/37. From left to right, standing: J.A. Lloyd, L. Lewis, Garfield Evans, W. Fry, Ron Griffiths, David Richards, Percy Williams. Seated: Clifford Edwards, Gwyn Evans, Lynwood Williams, D. Williams, G. Williams, E. Lewis.

Pontardawe Athletic AFC, 1960/61, the Welsh League Division 1 promotion winning side. From left to right, standing: S.G. Waltham (trainer), Richie Danahar, -?-, Ron Davies, Byron James, Alan Jones, Jimmy Drum, Jim Power, John Roberts (committee). Kneeling: Godfrey Evans, Mal Price, Gareth Humphries, Don Rothwell (captain), Ken Jenkins. Don Rothwell, born 1934 in Droylsden, Manchester, married a Gwaun-Cae-Gurwen girl and offered his services to the club. An ex-Manchester United colt he was one of the finest players to represent Pontardawe, playing between 1956 and 1972.

Pontardawe RFC, 1913. From left to right, back row, players: Lew Jones, Gwilym Michael, Jack ('Banker') Davies, Dan Jones (Clydach), Alec Williams, Tom ('Hong Kong') Jones (Clydach), Tom J. Williams ('Coch'), Trevor Rees. Middle: Fred Vaughan, Johnny Davies, Will Kift, Stanley Davies, W.J. Hopkin (Craigcefnparc). Front: Frank ('Talamis') Thomas, Owen Griffiths. The gentlemen, from left to right, standing at the back, are: Tom Jones, Frank Phillips, Billy Daniel, Aneurin Evans and Simon Daniel.

Pontardawe RFC charabanc, c. 1910. Outside the Cross Hotel, about to set off for a match against the 'Scarlets', is Pontardawe rugby team. They sit in 'The Franson' the first charabanc to be used in the valley, owned by Lewis W. Francis of Francis Motors. He bought it from Ford of Dagenham, in kit form, and assembled it at his garage at 12 High Street. It was capable of 12mph. The boy scout on the pavement is George Chilcott and the player wearing a jersey in the front seat is Dai Morgan from Alltwen. Other players are Dai Davies (Rhos), Graham Morgan, Will Morgan, Aneurin Evans and Fred Vaughan. Among the onlookers are David Jones (Alltycham Drive) and Willie Thomas (Herbert Street). In front of the bonnet is the driver, Dai Davies of Church Street.

Jack Carney (left) and Rex Williams before their British Youth Snooker Championship match in 1950/51. Born in 1932 'on top of a billiard hall' Jack Carney was destined to be a snooker player, starting to play when eight years of age. His father, John, himself a well known sporting personality in the locality was a great source of encouragement for the young Jack who learnt his craft in Dai Matthews' Billiard Hall, Herbert Street. He won the Welsh Boys and Youth Championship of Wales every year between 1947 and 1952, a feat never achieved since. In 1949/50 he went on to win the British Youth Snooker Championship defeating Ray Reardon in the final. He was defeated in the same championship in 1951 and 1952 by Rex Williams. He also played Fred Davis, then world snooker champion, in Pembroke Dock when stationed there as part of his national service.

Pontardawe Institute billiards team, winners of the West Wales League Championship, 1947/48. From left to right, standing: Norman Edwards, Richie Smith, Jackie Carney, Gwyn Harries. Seated: Arthur Hapgood, Gilbert Davies (captain) and Cyril W. Griffiths.

Thirteen
Images of Wartime

The Cenotaph, c. 1935. The cenotaph is situated at the junction of Holly Street with Herbert Street in front of the entrance to the former Pontardawe Public Hall and Institute. It was designed by Glendinning Moxham, a Swansea architect and sculpted by T.H. Jones. It originally commemorated the 106 men who fell in the First World War but another panel was added after the Second World War listing the 56 men killed during that conflict. The memorial was unveiled at the end of August 1921 and described by the *West Wales Observer* as follows: 'Holly and Herbert Streets were never so packed as on this occasion. On the corner of the streets and in Laurel Cottage garden a stand had been erected by the committee and this was occupied by the mothers and widows of the heroes. The service opened with the singing of "O God, our Help in Ages Past". The Rev. D.G. Jones, pastor of Soar Chapel, then offered up prayer in Welsh, whilst the Rev. Joel J. Davies (vicar) followed by reading a portion of scripture. Col. Watts Morgan unveiled the monument. Perfect silence prevailed during the sounding of the *Last Post* by buglers P. Hennesey, S. Price and T.J. Mainwaring and the playing of the *Dead March* by the band. The Male Voice Party sang *The Crusaders* and during the beautiful rendition, Mrs C.G. Gilbertson of Gellygron stepped forward and placed a large laurel wreath on the monument as a token of respect from the inhabitants of Pontardawe and District. This was one of the most moving and touching incidents during the ceremony.'

Unusual scene at Pontardawe, *c.* 1920. What is a field gun doing in The Castle yard? Local residents referred to this weapon as the cannon. Artillery pieces such as this were sold as scrap metal by the Ordnance Board at the end of the First World War. Many blacksmiths and farmers purchased the guns to obtain good quality wheels. The rest of the gun would be destined for the steelworks as scrap metal. Also depicted is St Peter's church, the brewery, and Gravel Bank House (left). The buildings on the right belong to the blacksmiths' shop. High Street Garage and other commercial premises occupy the site today.

Major Brinley Richard Lewis, killed in action on the Ypres front, 2 April 1917 aged twenty-six. One of four Pontardawe RFC players who have represented Wales at full international level, Brinley Lewis obtained his Welsh caps against Ireland in 1912 and 1913. On the second of his appearances he scored two dazzling tries, running fifty yards and leaving the full back stranded with that famous swerve of his on both occasions. E.H.D. Sewell in *The Rugby Football Internationals Rolls of Honour*, (London, 1919), wrote of him: 'He had splendid hands, true football pace, pluck, neat kicking ability…He was the best wing of his day in Wales who could boast only a couple of International caps.' His family owned the Glantawe tinplate works and his nephew is Bryn Lewis who ran an accountancy business in High Street, Pontardawe, for many years.

Crew of HMS *Courageous* under the main armament during the First World War. John Williams of Rhos is on the front row, second from left. He was born in Holly Street, Pontardawe but after marriage lived at Penparc, Rhos. John worked as a rollerman at W. Gilbertson & Co. but enlisted in the Royal Navy in 1914. He served on a number of ships after training before being posted to HMS *Courageous* in 1916. The latter was completed on 5 February 1916 as a light battle cruiser of 19,300 tons armed with four fifteen-inch guns. Both John and the ship survived the war.

PONTARDAWE RURAL DISTRICT COUNCIL

AIR RAID PRECAUTIONS

The following is an Official Statement of the Scheme of the Council in regard to Air Raid Precautions. The Public are earnestly requested to retain this Sheet for future reference or guidance.

WARNING SIGNALS:

Official warning of approach of Aircraft will be given on Works Hooters and Syrens by a succession of intermittent blasts of about 5 seconds separated by silent periods of 3 seconds duration. Official signal of ''Raid Over'' or ''Raiders Passed'' will be given by a continuous blast of 2 minutes duration at a steady pitch. N.B.—Preliminary or caution warnings will not be conveyed to the Public.

HEADQUARTERS:

The main A.R.P. Headquarters for all purposes is situated at the Old Brewery, High Street, Pontardawe. Telephone Number: Pontardawe 3170.

AIR RAID WARDEN SERVICE:

A Chief Air Raid Warden has been appointed for the whole of the Rural District (address, Council Offices, Pontardawe; Telephone: No. 136). In turn the district has been divided into 5 groups, each of which has an Air Raid Warden in charge. These groups have been further divided into sectors and each sector comprising of one or more streets requires a Sector Warden. The following Schedule will illustrate the Grouping and Sectors:—

Group No.	District.	No. of Sectors.	Group Air Raid Warden.	Address.
1.—Clydach, Craigcefnparc and Velindre		17	T. S. Lambert	Park Road, Clydach
2.—Pontardawe, Trebanos, Rhydyfro, Alltwen, Rhos, Ynysmudw, Gelly nadd and Clydebyll		25	S. O. Evans	34 Brecon Road, Pontardawe
3.—Ystalyfera, Godre'rgraig and Lower Cwmtwrch		14	Jenkin Evans	''Glen Hall,'' Ystalyfera
4.—Cwmllynfell, Rhiwfawr and Brynamman		6	P. C. B. Evans	Bryn Cwmllynfell
5.—Gwaun-cae-gurwen, Cwmgorse, Tai'rgwaith and Garnswllt		11	D. P. Rees	7 Carmel Street, Gwaun-cae-gurwen

VOLUNTEERS are required in each Group and in each Sector, and all persons who are prepared to offer their services should present themselves without delay to the Group Warden in their district, direct to the Chief Air Raid Warden, Council Offices, Pontardawe.

FIRST AID POSTS:

CLYDACH	PONTARDAWE	YSTALYFERA	GWAUN-CAE-GURWEN
Church Hall, Brook Street	Girls' School, Brecon Road.	Zoar Chapel Schoolroom	Infants' School

WOMEN HAVING HAD ANY EXPERIENCE OF NURSING, etc., TO ACT AS VOLUNTEERS ARE URGENTLY REQUIRED, AND PERSONS DESIR-ING TO ASSIST SHOULD CALL UPON OR COMMUNICATE WITH THE MEDICAL OFFICER OF HEALTH, COUNCIL OFFICES, PONTARDAWE.

PUBLIC SHELTERS:

CLYDACH, GLAIS, CRAIGCEFNPARC, VELINDRE.	PONTARDAWE, ALLTWEN, TREBANOS, YNYSMUDW.	GODRE'RGRAIG, PANTEG AND YSTALYFERA.
1—Trench, Tanyrallt Road, Clydach	1—G. W. Railway Tunnel, Uplands	1—Colliery Level, Old Pentwyn Colliery, opp. Godre'rgraig Park
2—Colliery Level, Bowen's Yard, near British Legion Club, Pontardawe Road	2—Cellar, Ellis' Shop, Herbert Street	2—Colliery Level, Pontycran, near Pentallwn
3—Trench, Hospital, Quarr Road	3—Archway over Clydach River, James Street	3—Colliery Level, near Cwmtawe-Gunol Farm
4—Colliery Level, Graigfelyn Colliery, Lone Road	4—Trench, Bronywawr Road	4—Colliery Level, Bottom of Clee's Lane, Panteg
5—Llwyndu Level, Glais	5—Colliery Level, Ynisfechan, off Ynysderw Road (near Chemical Works)	5—Colliery Level, Pwllbach, Ystalyfera
6—Elim Chapel, Craigcefnparc	6—Chapel Buildings, Alltwen Chapel	6—Colliery Tunnel, Pwllbach, Ystalyfera
	7—School Buildings, Dyffryn Road	7—Colliery Drift, Tirbach, Ystalyfera
	8—School Buildings, Trebanos Mixed School	
	9—Arches, Girls' School, Ynysmudw	

Air raid precautions for Pontardawe and district, 1938. This document was distributed to the public and reveals that the government and local authority were preparing for war in 1938. The air raid precautions were organised into wardens' districts with first aid posts and air-raid shelters in each district. The headquarters of the ARP was the brewery in Pontardawe. Public air-raid shelters were specially erected for the civilian population but large cellars were also utilised in a number of properties around Pontardawe. Air-raid shelters were built in the railway tunnel at The Uplands, under the river bridge at the Cross and at the Zinc School, Ynysmeudwy. The arches in the Pontardawe Girls' School were also used.

Sergeant Howard Griffiths, MM, was a member of the First Battalion of the Welsh Guards. He was stationed in Gibraltar when war was declared in September 1939 but was soon transferred with his battalion to Marseilles and then to the front line in northern France. Sgt Griffiths was stationed around the town of Arras in June 1940 when it was attacked and where he won his military medal (see below). He was wounded in action in 1940 and was captured by the Nazis when Arras was overrun. He spent some time in hospital before being taken to prisoner of war camps in Germany and Poland. Towards the end of the war Sgt Griffiths, together with fellow prisoners, was forced to walk from Oberselissir in Poland to Bavaria, a distance of some 800 miles, the journey taking over four months to complete (20 January to 22 April 1945). He was freed in May 1945 and returned home to his family in Heathfield Road, Pontardawe. He later owned a fish and chip shop at 52 High Street.

BUCKINGHAM PALACE.

I greatly regret that I am unable to give you personally the award which you have so well earned. I now send it to you with my congratulations and my best wishes for your future happiness.

George R.I.

2734193 Sjt. D.H. Griffiths, M.M.,
Welsh Guards.

Godfrey Penderel (1892-1943), 1931. Born at Garth Farm, Godfrey was one of four Penderel brothers. He fought in both world wars and had an adventurous career during both war and peace. He was badly wounded in the Dardanelles in 1915 while serving in the 4th Welsh Regiment. By the next year he had been transferred to the Royal Flying Corps. In 1931 he commanded the first flight of Vickers-Victoria troop-carrying planes through Africa from Nairobi to Capetown, a 6,000 mile journey which took three weeks, involving constant forced landings due to heavy rain storms. In 1933, along with Count Almazy (of *The English Patient* fame), he discovered rock paintings in the granite caves of the Libyan desert estimated to be 6,000 years old. He was killed in 1943 when his plane, involved in highly secret test flights, exploded.

Reunion of evacuees, 1999. At the start of the Second World War children were evacuated to the Pontardawe area from Chatham, Liverpool, Birmingham and London. They arrived, bewildered, with name labels, gas masks and small bags or cases. They were centred at Ynysderw House and greeted by Ailsa Evans-Semple and her helpers. From left to right, back row: Iris Clegg, Charles Carter, Don Phillips, Alf Smith. Middle: Pam Drummond, Margaret King, Ailsa Evans-Semple, Maureen Greenaway, Ann Carter, Pat Brunt. Front: Veronica Doyley, Joan Drapper.

Ambulance drivers, c. 1940. Left to right, back row: -?-, Peggy Humphries, -?-, Maggie Williams, Katie James, Una Rees. Front: Letty McNamara, -?-. The drivers worked in Swansea during the 'Three Nights' Blitz' of 19-21 February 1941.

In 1939, following the outbreak of war, the steel and tinplate manufacturers of the area received orders for the war effort, the works' themselves becoming targets for the Luftwaffe. When in 1937 the government introduced the Air Raid Precautions Act making ARP obligatory, teams of fire fighters were set up to combat the threat of bombing. Pictured is one such team established at Pontardawe steelworks. By today's standards the equipment looks primitive but it was probably used as an emergency unit until the fire brigade arrived to deal with any large conflagration.

'Register of Property Damaged by Enemy Action'. Pontardawe suffered two air raids during the Second World War on 21 October 1940 and 8 April 1941. The 1940 raid was part of a larger bombing mission over south Wales. The 1941 air raid was targeted at the Mumbles area but rumours persist in Pontardawe that the aircraft jettisoned their incendiary bombs on Pontardawe after failing to bomb Mumbles. The target could have been the steelworks at Pontardawe which was supplying steel to the Admiralty and War Office. The 1940 damage was caused by a large bomb or land mine which dropped on the fields above the foundry. The 1941 raid comprised fire bombs, which mostly dropped in Alltycham woods and Brynheulog. Only one property was totally destroyed – the Workingmen's Club in Church Street.

PONTARDAWE RURAL DISTRICT COUNCIL

REGISTER OF PROPERTY DAMAGED BY ENEMY ACTION

AIR RAID 21 OCTOBER 1940

Address	Damage	Cause
Main Road Ynysmeudwy	Shop window damaged	Bomb blast
Old Road Ynysmeudwy	Slates damaged on roof	Bomb blast

AIR RAID 8 APRIL 1941

Address	Damage	Cause
Bronywawr Road	Plaster damage to ceiling	Gunfire
Infants school	Roof damage	Incendiary bomb
2 Church Street	Roof damage	Incendiary bomb
9 Church Street	Roof damage	Incendiary bomb
22 Church Street	Roof damage	Incendiary bomb
31 Church Street	Roof damage	Incendiary bomb
James Street	Roof damage	Incendiary bomb
Church Street Working Men's Club Billiard room and main hall	Gutted	Incendiary bomb
Bar room	Damaged	
Uplands	Roof damage	Incendiary bomb
Pavilion Cinema	Roof damage	Incendiary bomb
Alltycham Road	Roof damage	Incendiary bomb

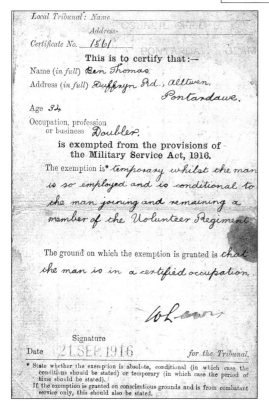

Many of the men working for W. Gilbertson & Co. during the First World War were in 'Certified Occupations' and were issued with 'Certificates of Exemption' under the Military Service Act 1916. Such exemptions were usually temporary while a man was employed in his certified occupation and was conditional upon him joining and remaining a member of the Volunteer Regiment.

Home Guard at Pontardawe during the Second World War. The event was one of the many fund-raising campaigns organised by the government to raise money to sustain the war effort. The Home Guard is on duty as part of this campaign but also as an honour guard for visiting dignitaries. Mr William John Evans of Pontardawe is the soldier in the front rank, first left. He was born in 1895 and employed in the steelworks. He was probably too old for active service at that time or was not called up for military service because he worked in a reserved occupation. He and his companions originally practised with broom sticks because of the acute shortage of rifles.

National Savings Campaign, during the Second World War. Nearly every community in Britain saved money to contribute toward the war effort by buying National Saving Certificates or War Bonds. A savings committee was formed in most towns to co-ordinate the work of fund raising. Pontardawe paid for two tanks in the 'Tanks for Attack' campaign of 1942 and several hurricane aircraft in the 'Wings for Victory' campaign in 1943. Smaller communities such as Rhos, Ynysmeudwy, Rhyd-y-fro, Trebanos and Alltwen were awarded certificates for their support to the savings campaigns.

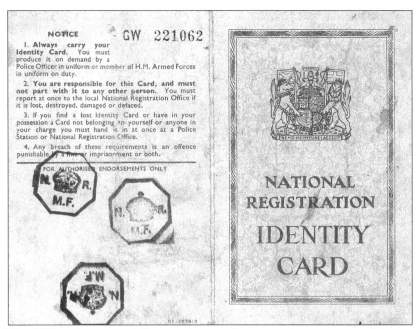

Second World War identity card. During the war the national registration of the population was undertaken as a security measure, every person being issued with an identity card. The latter had to be carried at all times and had to be produced on demand if so requested by a police officer in uniform or a member of the armed forces in uniform and on duty.

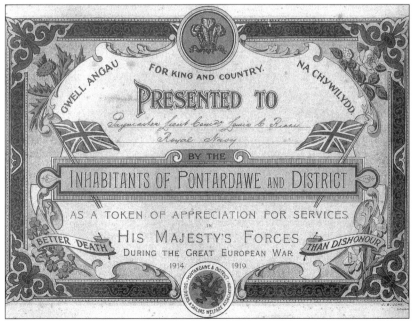

Certificate of appreciation devised by the Pontardawe & District Soldiers & Sailors Welfare Association and presented by the 'Inhabitants of Pontardawe and District' to those who served in His Majesty's Forces from the locality during 'The Great European War'. This certificate was presented to Paymaster Lieutenant Commander Lewis da Costa Ricci (see p. 54), Royal Navy. Note the motto, 'Better Death Than Dishonour'.

Acknowledgements

Special acknowledgements to:

Dafydd Rowlands for kindly agreeing to write the foreword; Michael Ritchie for supplying the photographic material regarding his ancestors, the Lewises of Brynheulog, and for comments and suggestions on the accompanying text; Susan Beckley, County Archivist, West Glamorgan Archive Service, for allowing the reproduction of the Bryn Seion chapel image on p. 82 and the interior of Tabernacle Independent chapel on p. 84; Revd Gareth Morgan Jones, Minister of Tabernacle, Alltwen and Bethesda Independent chapels and Revd Eirion Phillips, Minister of Gellionen Unitarian chapel and Capel-y-Graig, Trebanos; Marilyn Jones, Local Studies Librarian, Swansea Central Library, for her help with sources for the Lewises of Brynheulog and those relating to William 'Ivander' Griffiths (p. 101); the Ministry of Defence for permitting the reproduction of the RAF photograph on p. 2; the National Museums & Galleries of Wales for permission to reproduce the photograph on p. 47 (top); Neath Port Talbot County Borough Council, Technical and Property Services Directorate, for allowing reproduction of the images on pp 30 (top), and 46; the Ordnance Survey for giving permission for the reproduction of the maps on pp 12, 13, 39 and 51; Jane Friel, Regional Editor, Tempus Publishing Limited, for her encouragement and support.

Photographs, other images and information supplied by:

Mrs L. Bailey; Gwyneth Canning; Jack Carney; Brenda Davies; David Davies; Glenville Davies; Pam Davies; Wynne Davies; Huw and Mary George; Cissie Getvoldsen; Haydn Gibbon; Hannag Gittus; Miriam Gould; David Griffiths; John Griffiths; Nan Griffiths; Eddie Hanford; Elfed Harris; Edwin Hartland; Betty Hopkin; Bill and Hanna James; Anna Rhidwen James; Robert and Danny James; David Jenkins; William Jenkins; Hywel John; Bob Jones; Mr and Mrs Gareth Jones; Dorothy Jones; Margaret Jones (Gummery); Philip Jones; Raymond Jones; Annie Zena Lewis; Gwen Lewis; Jeff and June Lewis; Phyllis Lewis; Malcolm Lloyd; Audrey Melnick; Danny Morgan; Mary Morgan; Jenny Morris; National Assembly of Wales, Air Photograph Unit; Raymond Owen; R.M.S. Owen; Ann Petherick-Lewis; Derek Powell; Gwen Pugh; Deborah Rees; Teifion Rees; Nicholas Ritchie; J. Owen Roberts; Don Rothwell; Dorothy Stockden; Swansea Valley Historical Society; Melville Thomas; Norman Thomas; A.J. Watkins; Gerald Williams; Gordon Williams; Mair Williams; Mair Williams.

Other information and assistance from:

Aladdin Industries Ltd; Bairdwear Ltd; D. Bennett; B. Bowen; Broadhaven Nursing Home; G. Cadwalladr; H. and J. Childs; V. Cirillo; A. Clayton; K. Collis; Companies House, Cardiff; M. Cunningham; Cwm Cartref Nursing Home; D.J. Davies; G. Davies; S. Doyle; H. Ebenezer; Economic Packaging Ltd; B. Edwards; J. Edwards; D. Evans; Pastor J. Evans; J. Evans; Hubert Gibbon; M. Gibbs; D.J. Griffiths; Dr R. Griffiths; Mr and Mrs A. Hayward; G. Hicks; B. Hilbourne; E. Hopkin; J. Hopkin; D. Howells; E. Howells; R. Howells; W. Hudson; E. James; P. James; R. Jenkins; Mrs M. Jeremiah; A. John; E.H. John; A. Jones; J.R. Jones; N. Jones; R. Jones; M. Kidwell; R. Lanchbury; Pastor J. Langford; Lidl Foodstores; T. Lloyd; Matthews Building and Commercial Services Ltd; Mid and West Wales Fire Authority; H. Middleton; J. Morris; R. Morris; Mr and Mrs W.J. Morris; A.P. Mouls; National Association of Retired Fire-Fighters, Mid and West Wales Branch; the National Library of Wales; R. Osborne; R. Perkins; Prof. G.O. Pierce; Pontardawe International Music Festival; Pontardawe Leisure Centre; Pontardawe Library; A. Rees; S. Rees; P. Reynolds; A. Saunders; Somerfield's; *South Wales Evening Post*; *South Wales Guardian*; Spar Store, Alltwen; C. Steadman; S. Steadman; S. Sutton; B. Thomas; B. Thomas; I. Thomas; J. Thomas; L. Thomas; R. Thomas; Trebanos RFC; N. Watkins; Welsh Development Agency; Pastor G. Weeks; E. Williams; Pastor G. Williams; A.G. Williams; H. Williams; P. Williams; S. Williams; W.J. Williams; J. Wilson.